CHOOSING A VOCATION

by

Frank Parsons

A Reprint of the Original 1909
Book with an Introduction by
Carl McDaniels,
NVGA President 1973-1974

This is a complete reprint of the original book by Frank Parsons who played such an important early role in developing the field of career guidance.

Published and distributed by the
    National Career Development Association
    305 North Beech Circle
    Broken Arrow, OK 74012

    Phone: (918) 663-7060
    Fax: (918) 663-7058
    www.ncda.org

Parsons, Frank, 1854-1908.
    Choosing a vocation / by Frank Parsons.
        p. cm.
    "A reprint of the original 1900 book with an introduction by Carl McDaniels."
    ISBN-13: 978-1-885333-14-8
    ISBN-10: 1-885333-14-5 (pbk.)
    1. Occupations. 2. Vocational guidance. I. Title.

HF5381.P24 2005
331.702--dc22

                             2005056220

PREFACE

Many writers in the career development field like to talk about how things are drastically changing and how our work requires a whole new way of thinking and engaging with the clients we serve. While some things have indeed changed, the fundamental propositions put forward by Frank Parsons are still relevant today. Frank Parsons was a man ahead of his time with respect to capturing the essentials of the career guidance process, and reaching out to a broad spectrum of individuals who could benefit from career services. It is with great pride that the National Career Development Association issues a reprint of Parsons' seminal work, *Choosing a Vocation*. In the career development field, the past inevitably influences our present-day work, and Parsons' contributions stand as a monument to that tenet. By understanding where we came from as a profession, we are better informed to shape our future.

Janet G. Lenz,
NCDA President, 2004-2005

iv

INTRODUCTION

It is a signal honor to introduce this edition of Frank Parsons' classic work, *Choosing a Vocation*. This reprint of his original work recognizes the 80th anniversary of its first publication in 1909 and highlights the recognition he is receiving this year from the guidance community.

For many career counselors, however, the name "Frank Parsons" is shrouded in mystery. True, he is cited in the literature as the "father of vocational guidance" in much the same way that his chronological counterparts Henry Ford and the Wright Brothers are given credit for the development of the automobile and the airplane. But, too little is known about Frank Parsons today and the need to fill that void prompted the republication of this book.

Frank Parsons was born in Mount Holly, New Jersey on November 14, 1854. Indeed, when he was born there were many who had lived fully as long as the "United States of America." At the age of 15, Parsons enrolled in Cornell University and graduated three years later with a degree in engineering. More important, perhaps, than his engineering degree was the encouragement Parsons received at Cornell to try new ideas and the good that they can create for people. The young Parsons went to work in the railroad industry but his career was cut short by the depression of 1873 and he was forced to work as a laborer. As conditions improved, he located a job teaching art, mathematics, history, and French in Southbridge, Massachusetts.

After teaching six years, Parsons accepted the urgings

of a local judge to take up the study of law with him, the customary method of preparing for the field in those days. For the next few years, he pursued his legal studies and in 1881 passed the Massachusetts bar examination with what were reportedly the highest scores in 12 years. This was also the midpoint of Parsons' life and he was yet to enter the field for which he is known today.

Parsons practiced law for a number of years and even made an unsuccessful try at running for mayor of Boston. He taught law courses for many years at Boston University and for this reason was often referred to as "Professor Parsons" in his later years.

In the late 1890s, Parsons taught for two years at what is now Kansas State University and at the short-lived Ruskin College in Missouri. He maintained his teaching ties with Boston University, however, even while in the midwest.

The turn of the century heralded an intensive period of innovation and publication which established his role in the history of guidance in the United States. Between 1905 and his untimely death at age 54 on September 26, 1908, Parsons turned his full attention to developing the core of the vocational guidance movement in Boston. He had packed an eventful career lifetime into his first years— engineer, laborer, high school teacher, lawyer, politician, professor, author—and now used this to help young people and adults to make intelligent career choices. Many might consider him unqualified to counsel, based upon today's standards. But, in those days, there were no undergraduate courses in tests and measurements or personnel techniques or graduate programs in counseling and guidance.

Parsons wanted to influence and be a part of the social, economic, and political changes going on in his era. He was a passionate and active participant in the events of his day. For many in America, life was hard and suitable work was both difficult to obtain and difficult to execute. Given the rigors of life it was far too glib to refer to the 1890s as the

"Gay 90s" and too easy to lose track of the plight of most Americans while the media was euphoric over "America's emergence as a world power" after the successful (from our standpoint) Spanish American War. Consider the facts that Frank Parsons worked before personnel departments began to spring up in American businesses in the 1910s, before a few dozen counselors met to form the first guidance association in 1913, before Social Security emerged in the 1930s to give many a reasonable chance for a life after work, and before the expansion of higher education in the 1940s greatly increased chances for upward mobility in our society.

But, back to Boston at the turn of the century. The settlement house movement was in full swing when the Civic Service House was opened in Boston in 1901. Shortly after, Parsons was invited to head up a sort of workers institute. Today, we might call it a continuing education center but then it was graced with the more earthy "Breadwinner's Institute." Between 1905 and 1908, hundreds of adults passed through its doors and a high proportion were aided in the process. Based upon the success of this effort, in January 1908 Parsons renamed the institute the "Vocational Bureau of the Civic Service House." It was privately funded. His work at the Bureau led to Parsons' book—this book—*Choosing a Vocation*, which was actually published in 1909 after his death.

For those interested in more details on Parsons' life, two highly recommended works are *Frank Parsons— Prophet, Innovator, Counselor* by Howard V. Davis (a book published in 1969 by the Southern Illinois University Press) and "The Counselor as a Prophet: Frank Parsons, 1854-1908" by Richard M. Gummere, Jr. (an article which appeared in the May 1988 issue of the *Journal of Counseling and Development*).

Looking back over time, one can easily sense that Parsons' ideas, his methods, and his concern for career development for all people represent thinking far beyond the scope of his day and provided a framework modified over the years by counselors to focus their work today. Here are a few examples selected from this book.

1. An emphasis on the scientific method in career decision making. (Chapter 1)
2. A clear statement of purpose:
   "In the wise choice of a vocation, there are three broad factors: (1) a clear understanding of yourself, your aptitudes, abilities, interests, ambitions, resources, limitations, and their causes; (2) a knowledge of the requirements and conditions of success, advantages and disadvantages, compensation, opportunities, and prospects in different lines of work; (3) true reasoning in the relations of these two groups of facts." (page 5)
3. A clear outline of how to proceed with the purpose of vocational guidance in a logical method (Chapter 5)
4. A logical classification of industries. (Chapter 7)
5. A proposed counselor preparation program. (Chapter 13)
6. A series of case studies for those who want illustrations. (Chapter 15)
7. Finally, for those who want to be reassured about the concept that individuals should be allowed to make their own decisions, Parsons has this to say:
   "The Bureau does not attempt to decide for any boy what occupation he should choose, but aims to help him investigate the subject and come to a conclusion on his own account, that is much more likely to be valid and useful than if no effort were made to apply scientific methods to the problem. Our mottoes are Light, Information, Inspiration, Cooperation." (page 92)

I invite a new generation of counselors to share in the joy and inspiration by reading Frank Parsons in the original. Read for the big ideas. Try not to focus on some of the gender problems and the few peculiar approaches of

Parsons. Read *Choosing a Vocation* in the context of 1908 and see how much of it makes sense to you today. Search diligently for the long term truths and the meaning and application of Parsons' ideas to your work today. For your reading, I wish you a full measure of the vision, forethought, and compelling sense of good will toward all people which characterizes the work of Frank Parsons.

March 1989   Carl McDaniels
                      Professor of Counselor Education
                      Virginia Tech
                      Blacksburg, Virginia

x

POST SCRIPT

It is a pleasure to add a brief post script to my Introduction of the 1989 reprinting of the Parsons' book. First, my thanks to NCDA member Bob Calvert, long time Editor of Garrett Park Press for having the courage to publish the second reprinting of *Choosing a Vocation*. The first reprinting was done in 1967 by Agathon Press in New York. Second, it is indeed a joyous occasion for me to see the pioneering work of Frank Parsons being reprinted by the National Career Development Association. Parsons' 1909 book filled with key concepts for our new field set the stage for the founding of the National Vocational Association in 1913 in Grand Rapids, Michigan, after there had been a preliminary organizational meeting in 1910 in Parsons' home city of Boston, MA. It seems to me the National Career Development Association and Frank Parsons' work have finally been joined together almost 100 years later. My deep appreciation to the Publications Development Council and the NCDA Board of Directors for their creative and forward thinking in bringing our professional association and this seminal book together as each one approaches a centennial celebration.

August 2005
Carl McDaniels
NVGA President 1973-1974

xii

DEDICATION

To Mrs. Quincy A. Shaw, the progressive daughter of Agassiz, whose far-sighted and beneficent philanthropy has done so much for the young people of Boston, and indirectly through the spread of her institutions, for young people throughout the country, this book is dedicated in a spirit of reverent affection and respect.

INTRODUCTORY NOTE

THE manuscript of this book was practically ready for publication when Professor Parsons died. For a year prior to his death he had given a large part of his time to Vocation Bureau work. Some of the material here used appeared in articles in *The Arena*, and a number of the "cases" in Part III have been published in the daily papers of Boston and New York. The appearance of these articles brought hundreds of letters of inquiry from all parts of the United States, expressing interest in the effort to give scientific vocational counsel to the young. That Professor Parsons would have carried the plan to a greater completeness had he lived, there is no doubt; but the work that he did do is of such value that it is believed many will be grateful to get such information about it as can be given in this volume.

Whatever doubts there may be of the practicability of giving expert vocational counsel to young men and women, there are certain simple truths upon which the plan is based, and which I believe no one will deny.

1. It is better to choose a vocation than merely to "hunt a job."

2. No one should choose a vocation without careful self-analysis, thorough, honest, and under guidance.

3. The youth should have a large survey of the field of vocations, and not simply drop into the convenient or accidental position.

4. Expert advice, or the advice of men who have made a careful study of men and of vocations and of the

conditions of success, must be better and safer for a young man than the absence of it.

5. *Putting it down* on paper seems to be a simple matter, but it is one of supreme importance in this study. No young man can make the self-analysis which Professor Parsons calls for *on paper* without gaining a distinct benefit, a guide, a rudder, a plan which will reduce very greatly his liability to become a mere piece of driftwood upon the industrial sea.

A thoughtful reading of the "cases" in Part III will give the reader a fair test of the practical application of the plan and its freedom from dogmatism or any undue claim to the word "scientific." In practical helpfulness to the scores of people who have applied to the Bureau it has established its worth and its sanity; and I am convinced that it will be reproduced in other communities, and eventually, in its fundamental principles, in our educational system itself.

RALPH ALBERTSON.

BOSTON, May 1, 1909.

CONTENTS

PART I. THE PERSONAL INVESTIGATION

    I. The Importance of Scientific Method 3

    II. The Principles and Methods Involved 5

    III. Counselors and Applicants 14

    IV. Extended Discussion of Personal Data 26

    V. The Method in Outline 47

PART II. THE INDUSTRIAL INVESTIGATION

    VI. The Conditions of Efficiency and Success in Different Industries 49

    VII. Classifications of Industries 65

    VIII. Industries Open to Women 66

    IX. The Use of Statistics 71

    X. The Movement of the Demand for Workers . . . 74

    XI. The Geographical Distribution of Workers . . 83

PART III. THE ORGANIZATION AND THE WORK

    XII. The Vocation Bureau 89

    XIII. The School for Vocational Counselors 91

    XIV. Supplementary Helps 94

    XV. Sample Cases 109

    XVI. Conclusions 160

PART I

THE PERSONAL INVESTIGATION

I

THE IMPORTANCE OF SCIENTIFIC METHOD

No step in life, unless it may be the choice of a husband or wife, is more important than the choice of a vocation. The wise selection of the business, profession, trade, or occupation to which one's life is to be devoted and the development of full efficiency in the chosen field are matters of the deepest moment to young men and to the public. These vital problems should be solved in a careful, scientific way, with due regard to each person's aptitudes, abilities, ambitions, resources, and limitations, and the relations of these elements to the conditions of success in different industries.

If a boy takes up a line of work to which he is adapted, he will achieve far greater success than if he drifts into an industry for which he is not fitted. An occupation out of harmony with the worker's aptitudes and capacities means inefficiency, unenthusiastic and perhaps distasteful labor, and low pay; while an occupation in harmony with the nature of the man means enthusiasm, love of work, and high economic values, — superior product, efficient service, and good pay. If a young man chooses his vocation so that his best abilities and enthusiasms will be united with his daily work, he has laid the foundations of success and happiness. But if his best abilities and enthusiasms are separated from his daily work, or do not find in it fair scope and opportunity for exercise and development; if his occupation is merely a means of making a living, and the work he loves to do is side-tracked into the evening hours, or pushed out of his life altogether, he will be only a fraction of the man

4   CHOOSING A VOCATION

he ought to be. Efficiency and success are largely dependent on adaptation. A man would not get good results by using his cow to draw his carriage and his horse for dairy purposes; yet the difference of adaptability in that case is no more emphatic than the differences in the aptitudes, capacities, powers, and adaptabilities of human beings.

We guide our boys and girls to some extent through school, then drop them into this complex world to sink or swim as the case may be. Yet there is no part of life where the need for guidance is more emphatic than in the transition from school to work, — the choice of a vocation, adequate preparation for it, and the attainment of efficiency and success. The building of a career is quite as difficult a problem as the building of a house, yet few ever sit down with pencil and paper, with expert information and counsel, to plan a working career and deal with the life problem scientifically, as they would deal with the problem of building a house, taking the advice of an architect to help them.

Boys generally drift into some line of work by chance, proximity, or uninformed selection; and the high percentage of inefficiency and change experienced by many employers in their working force, and the cost it entails in employment expense, waste of training, and low-grade service, are largely due to the haphazard way in which young men and women drift into employments, with little or no regard to adaptability, and without adequate preparation, or any definite aim or well-considered plan to insure success.

The aim of this book is to point out practical steps that can be taken to remedy these conditions through expert counsel and guidance, in the selection of a vocation, the preparation for it, and the transition from school to work. No person may decide for another what occupation he should choose, but it is possible to help him so to approach the problem that he shall come to wise conclusions for himself.

II

THE PRINCIPLES AND METHODS INVOLVED

In the wise choice of a vocation there are three broad factors: (1) a clear understanding of yourself, your aptitudes, abilities, interests, ambitions, resources, limitations, and their causes; (2) a knowledge of the requirements and conditions of success, advantages and disadvantages, compensation, opportunities, and prospects in different lines of work; (3) true reasoning on the relations of these two groups of facts.

Every young person needs help on all three of these points. He needs all the information and assistance he can get. He needs counsel. He needs a vocational counselor. He needs careful and systematic help by experienced minds in making this greatest decision of his life.

The more light he can bring to bear on the problem from his own observation, reading, and experience, the better it will be for the clearness and strength of the conclusions arrived at, and the permanent value of the results attained. The first step, therefore, is self-study.

To win the best success of which one is capable, his best abilities and enthusiasms must be united with his daily work. He needs, therefore, to investigate himself in order to determine his capacities, interests, resources, and limitations, and their causes, so that he may compare his aptitudes, abilities, ambitions, etc., with the conditions of success in different industries.

The schedule of personal data outlined later in these pages may be used as part of the process of self-investigation and self-revelation. The answers the young man or

CHOOSING A VOCATION

woman makes to these questions afford much light on the problem under consideration, not only by their direct relations to it, but indirectly also; for a careful counselor can read between the lines a great deal about the accuracy, clearness, directness, and definiteness of thought, care, thoroughness, modesty or conceit, mental make-up, and special characteristics of the young man's character and ability. In addition to the schedule study, the counselor puts whatever questions and makes whatever tests the case may call for, on the general principle already stated.

When I hand this schedule to a young man I talk to him somewhat as follows: —

"Some of these questions can be answered very definitely. In respect to others, the character questions for example, you can only make estimates more or less imperfect and subject to revision. Some questions you may not be able to answer at all without assistance and careful testing. But do the best you can. Consider every question carefully, try to form a good judgment on it, and state the tests or evidence you rely on in making your judgment. A thorough study of yourself is the foundation of a true plan of life. Deal with the matter as though correct conclusions would mean ten thousand dollars to you. A true judgment of yourself may mean more than that. Stand off and look at yourself as though you were another individual. Look yourself in the eye. Compare yourself with others. See if you can remember as much as the best of your companions about a lecture or a play you have heard together, or a passage or book you have both read. Watch the people you admire, note their conduct, conversation, and appearance, and how they differ from people you do not admire. Then see which you resemble most. See if you are as careful, thorough, prompt, reliable, persistent, good-natured, and sympathetic as the best people you know. Get your friends to help you form true judgments about yourself, and, above all things, be on your guard against self-conceit and flattery. Test every element of your character, knowledge, mental power, appearance, manners, etc., as well as you can. And then bring the study to the counselor. He will help you revise it, make further tests, suggest the means of judging questions not yet satisfactorily

PRINCIPLES AND METHODS INVOLVED 7

answered, and consider with you the relations between your aptitude, abilities, etc., and the requirements, conditions of success, advantages and disadvantages, opportunities and prospects in the various callings you might engage in, and also consider the best means of preparation and advancement to secure the fullest efficiency and success in the field of work you may decide upon."

The study made by the applicant reveals much more to the counselor than is contained in the answers made to schedule points. He can read between the lines important messages as to care, accuracy, memory, clearness and definiteness of thought, directness or irrelevancy, conceit or modesty, common sense, etc., which help to indicate the suggestions that ought to be made in the individual case.

Besides this study by the applicant on his own account, the counselor usually questions him at some length in a private interview. Ancestry, family, education, reading, experience, interests, aptitudes, abilities, limitations, resources, etc., are inquired into with a vigor and directness that are not possible in a written research. The memory is tested and the general intelligence so far as possible, the senses also and delicacy of touch, nerve, sight, and hearing reactions, association-time, etc., where these facts appear to be important elements in the problem. For example, an artist needs, among other things, good visual memory and delicacy of touch; a dentist should have keen sight, delicate touch, correlation of hand and eye, and plenty of nerve; and if the verbal memory is defective or the auditory reactions are slow, it would probably be difficult to become a thoroughly expert stenographer. So again, slow sight and hearing reactions would be one indication against the probability of becoming highly expert as a telegrapher or a thoroughly competent chauffeur. The workers in some psychologic laboratories think the tests of reaction-time are liable to too much variation from special causes, difference in the stimulus, attention, emotional conditions, etc., to be of much practical value. But the Yale experiments on sight and hear-

CHOOSING A VOCATION

ing reactions seem to afford a clear basis for taking such facts into account in forming a rational judgment, and that is the opinion of a number of investigators of high authority. When the normal reactions, and the extreme reactions under intense stimulation and keen attention, are carefully tested and compared with the average results, the data certainly afford some light on the individual's probable aptitude and capacities. Other things equal, a girl with slow normal hearing reactions could not expect to become so readily and completely proficient in stenography as a girl whose normal reactions are unusually quick. Tests of association-time, memory-time, will-time, etc., may throw some light on the probability of developing power in cross-examination, executive ability, fitness to manage large affairs, etc. Rapidity and definiteness of memory and association, promptness and clearness of decision, etc., are certainly more favorable than their opposites to the development of the powers just mentioned. Nevertheless, it must not be forgotten that all such indications are only straws, hints to be taken into account with all the other facts of the case. The handicap of slow decision or imperfect memory may be more than overcome by superiority in industry, earnestness, vitality, endurance, common sense, sound judgment, etc.

For the purpose of aiding to get a comprehensive view of the field of opportunity, we have a classified list of more than two hundred ways in which women are earning money, and similar classified lists of industries for men. Another study has been made and is published herewith in regard to the conditions of success in different industries: first, the fundamentals, applicable in large measure to all industries; and second, the special conditions, applicable to particular industries or groups of industries. For example, health, energy, care, enthusiasm, reliability, love of the work, etc., are essential to the best success in any industry;

PRINCIPLES AND METHODS INVOLVED 9

while power of expression with the voice is peculiarly related to success in the ministry, law, and public life; organizing and executive ability, knowledge of human nature and ability to deal with it, power to manage men harmoniously and effectively, are important factors in business affairs of the larger sort; and delicacy of touch, coördination of hand and brain, fine sense of color, form, and proportion, strong memory for combinations of sound, etc., are special elements in artistic and musical success.

Opportunities, specific and general, in different lines of work should be classified with reference to each of the leading industries, and also with regard to the location of industrial centres of various sorts and the geographical distribution of demand. A table has been prepared showing all the leading industries in Massachusetts, with their relative development and geographical centres. Similar tables can be made for other states and for the United States. Attention is also given to the relative growth of industries and the movement of demand. For instance, census figures show that the per cent of progress in the printing trade in Massachusetts is four times the per cent of progress for the whole group of manufacturing and mechanical industries. Again, industrial education is growing very rapidly, and the demand for competent teachers of commercial branches and the mechanic arts, woodwork, machine work, etc., is much greater than the supply. As data develop on these lines, more and more complete and perfect information relating to immediate and specific openings and opportunities for employment, and to the general and permanent demand in different occupations, will be made available. Data in regard to pay, conditions of labor, chances of advancement, etc., should also be collected and systematized.

There is possibility here for coöperation with employment agencies of the right kind, with very valuable and helpful results.

10 CHOOSING A VOCATION

We have in tabular form the courses given in the leading vocational schools, and are making simple tables of all the day and evening courses in or near our city that have a vocational bearing, noting the length of each course, its beginning, time per day and week, age and conditions of admission, cost, opportunities of earning money while studying, etc., so that young men and women can see at a glance all the institutions that give such courses as they may desire and the relative advantage as to time, cost, and conditions.

Special effort is made to develop analytic power. The power to see the essential facts and principles in a book or a man or a mass of business data, economic facts, or political and social affairs, reduce these essentials to their lowest terms and group them in their true relations in brief diagrams or pictures, is invaluable in any department of life where clear thinking and intellectual grasp are important elements. This analytic power is one of the corner-stones of mastery and achievement. To develop it we give the student class of applicants samples of good analytic work, and ask them to read a good book and analyze it, or make an investigation and reduce the facts to analytic form. After they have had some practice in analysis, we use the following more extensive contract, which calls for a dozen items or such portions of them as the counselor may deem best to ask for.

In reading . . . . under agreement with the Vocation Bureau dated . . . . make a page or more of keynotes on the following points, and talk them over with the counselor for the mutual benefit of all concerned.

Put page reference after each point you note.

1. FACTS. The half-dozen facts that seem to you most important.
2. EVENTS. The leading events or landmarks of the book.
3. PRINCIPLES. The half-dozen principles you think most vital.

PRINCIPLES AND METHODS INVOLVED   11

4. CHARACTERS. The chief characters (if the book deals with characters) and their most striking characteristics.

5. IDEAS. The most interesting and inspiring ideas.

6. SUGGESTIONS. The most helpful suggestions and their application to your life.

7. BEAUTY, USE, HUMOR. Passages that are specially beautiful, novel, useful, or humorous.

8. INTERESTS AND REASONS. The things that interest you most of all, and the reasons they interest you.

9. ETHICS, MORALS. The ethical aspects, or right and wrong of the book and its characters, events, ideas, and principles.

10. COMMON SENSE. Criticisms as to purpose, method, make-up, style, etc. What you would say to the author if he asked you *(a)* how you liked the book, *(b)* what you liked best, *(c)* what you did n't like, and *(d)* how you think it could be improved.

11. COMPARISON, RANK. Comparison of the book with others you have read, and the rank you would give it.

12. APPLICATIONS. General utility of the book, — application of its facts, teachings, etc., to individuals, society, government, industry, civilization, etc.

I find it best to have at least fifteen minutes' private talk with the applicant before he begins his personal study (and half an hour or an hour is better still, if it can be had), in order to question him about his education, reading, and experience, how he spends his spare time and his money, the nature of his interests and ambitions, and the general outline of his problem. Sometimes the case is pretty clear at the first interview; sometimes a good deal of study is needed to get the right clue. If the boy is undeveloped and inexperienced and shows no special aptitudes, he is advised to read about various industries in Fowler's "Starting in Life" and other vocational books, and visit farms, factories, carpenter shops, machine shops, laboratories, electric works, railroad depots, buildings in course of construction,

12 CHOOSING A VOCATION

newspaper offices, photograph studios, courts, banks, stores, etc., talk with the workers and superintendents, too, if he can, try his hand at different sorts of work on the farm, in the care of animals, in the factory, office, and store, so as to get an experience sufficient to bring out his aptitudes and abilities, if he has any, and to form a basis for an intelligent judgment as to what he shall try to do in the world.

Breadth is important as well as specialization. A man cannot be fully successful, nor secure against the changes constantly occurring in industry, unless he knows a good deal besides the special knowledge immediately applicable to his business. There is no way in many cases to bring true interests and aptitudes into clear relief, except through variety of experience. An interest in a certain line of work, or the lack of interest, may be the result of knowledge or of ignorance, an indication of power or of weakness. A boy often takes a dislike to his father's occupation because he sees the inside of it and knows all its "outs," while he does not know the disadvantages of other occupations in respect to which he is familiar only with the outside. It may be that a wider experience will develop some new interest and aptitude, stronger than any that is now in evidence. Many boys might be equally successful either in business, or farming, or some mechanical line, or one of the professions. Any honorable work in which there was a fair chance for advancement would interest them after they had passed the initial stages and got sufficient skill and understanding of the calling to work with reasonable facility and certainty. In such cases the choice of an occupation is largely the question of opportunity and industrial demand. If the father, or uncle, or any relative or friend has a good business into which the boy can grow with a prospect of adaptation and efficiency, the burden of proof is on the proposition that this foundation should be abandoned and another building started on a new site. If there are excellent openings in forestry,

PRINCIPLES AND METHODS INVOLVED   13

scientific agriculture, business and office management, skillful art-craft, teaching the mechanical arts, etc., such facts must have full weight in cases where outside opportunity, East or West or South, is a determining factor. The question of resources, ability to take expensive courses of instruction and wait long years for remunerative practice or position, is also very important. But the fundamental question that outranks all the others is the question of adaptation, — the question of uniting, so far as may be possible, the best abilities and enthusiasms or the developed man with the daily work he has to do.

III

COUNSELORS AND APPLICANTS

I LIKE to begin with a general talk to a class or a club or some other organization or group of students or young people, presenting the matter in some such form as this: —

If you had a million dollars to invest, you would be very careful about it; you would study methods of investment, and get expert counsel and advice from those familiar with such things, and try to invest your money so it would be safe and would pay you good dividends. Your life is worth more than a million dollars to you. You would not sell it for that. And you are investing it day by day and week by week. Are you studying the different methods of investment open to you, and taking counsel to help you decide just what investment you had better make in order to get the best returns upon your capital?

The Vocation Bureau has been established to help you in this. One of the most important steps in life is the choice of an occupation. If you take up a line of work to which you are adapted or can adapt yourself, you are likely to be happy and successful. If a man loves his work and can do it well, he has laid the foundation for a useful and happy life. But if his best abilities and enthusiasms do not find scope in his daily work, if his occupation is merely a means of making a living, and the work he loves to do is side-tracked into the evening hours or pushed out of his life altogether, he will be only a fraction of the man he ought to be. Efficiency and success are largely dependent on adaptation. You must learn what you are best adapted to do, and get started in that line.

You may not be able to get into the right line of work at first. You may have to earn your living for a while in any way that is open to you. But if you study yourself and get sufficient knowledge of various industries to determine what sort of work you

COUNSELORS AND APPLICANTS   15

are best adapted to, and then carefully prepare yourself for efficient service in that line, the opportunity will come for you to make use of the best that is in you in your daily work.

Lincoln tried farming, lumbering, rail-splitting, and running a flat-boat. He was a teacher, postmaster, captain in the Black Hawk War, storekeeper and surveyor. But whatever he did to earn a living, he was always spending his spare time in reading good books and in telling stories and discussing public questions. He kept studying himself also, and he concluded that his special abilities were his great physical strength and his power to express himself in a forceful and attractive way which made people like to hear him talk. His bodily strength fitted him for such heavy work as blacksmithing, and he debated with himself whether he would learn that trade or the law. It would be comparatively easy to get a start in blacksmithing, for little capital would be required and he could earn his living probably at once, whereas it would cost much time and money to make himself a good lawyer and get practice enough to support him. While physical power and an easy open way invited him to blacksmithing, he knew that his higher powers — his distinguishing traits of mind and character — adapted him to public life and the law, and he obeyed the call in spite of the difficulties in the way. He found friends to help him in his studies and his entrance to civic life and legal practice. He was elected to the legislature of Illinois when he was twenty-five years old, and began the practice of law in Springfield when he was twenty-eight.

You know the rest; how he gradually built up a good practice, went to Congress, became a power in his state, and was chosen chief executive of the nation in 1860 at the age of fifty-one. If he had remained a storekeeper, or a surveyor, or a boatman, we probably never would have heard of him. He would have done his work well and made an honest living, and put his spare time into telling stories and discussing public questions with his neighbors. His best power and enthusiasm would have been separated from his work. They would have sought an outlet in his leisure hours, while his work would have been simply a means of earning a livelihood. He studied himself to find out and develop his best abilities, and persevered in preparing for and entering upon a field of usefulness in which his highest aptitudes, abili-

CHOOSING A VOCATION

ties, and enthusiasms could find full scope and expression and be united with his daily work, and that was one of the fundamental reasons for his great success.

Have *you* found out in what direction *your* chief abilities lie, in what line you are best adapted to achieve success, and the methods and principles to be followed in your upward progress? If not, is it not time you began to study yourself and your possibilities with a view to making a clear decision and building up a successful career in the calling to which your aptitudes, capacities, interests, and ambitions best adapt you?

Some of the cases that have come before the Bureau are then described, in order to show how the system works, and an invitation is given to any who desire a consultation to make an appointment with the counselor. Sometimes a considerable part of the audience responds to this invitation. After a talk to a class of thirty or forty boys, for example, the teacher and all the larger boys made appointments which kept the counselor busy for over two weeks.

Many applicants also come individually in response to the circulars that have been distributed, or press notices that have appeared from time to time.

The first interview with an applicant generally requires from fifteen minutes to an hour. I question him at sufficient length to get a general idea of his situation, sometimes asking him to write the answers to the questions in my presence, but more frequently noting the answers myself directly in my Vocation Register, a notebook of convenient size which I can easily carry about with me.

I begin by getting the name and address of the applicant, and then ask him to state his problem as briefly and concisely as possible, taking not more than one or two minutes in the recital. This frees his mind at the burning point, and makes him feel that you have got at the kernel of his difficulty at the start, so that he is more ready and willing than he otherwise would be to go through a careful questioning about all sorts of details which must follow if the counselor is to gain a thorough understanding of the case.

COUNSELORS AND APPLICANTS 17

The sole condition of this interview is that we shall be perfectly frank with each other. That is the only way in which we can get at the valuable results that are desired.

I use, as a rule, a course of questioning substantially as follows: —

Age?

Height?

Weight?

Health record? How much time have you lost from illness in the last two years? Five years? Ten years?

What tests of endurance have you undergone?

How far can you walk?

How much can you lift?

Is your digestion good?

Are there any hereditary diseases in your family? If so, what?

Where were you born?

What is your father's business? His father's business? The business of your mother's father? Of your uncles on both sides? Of your brothers, if you have any? The extent and importance of the business in each case? What opportunity have you to enter the business in each case? Are you drawn toward your father's business, your uncle's, etc., or do you dislike it? Will your father open the way for you to make a success in his line? Same with uncle, brother, etc.?

Sometimes the family bent toward a given line of work, teaching, for example, or mechanical industry, is so marked as to furnish one indication of the probable direction in which a young man's aptitudes may be found to lie. Sometimes, also, the opportunity for entering upon the business in which the father or brother or uncle is engaged is so excellent as to furnish a strong reason for carefully considering that course.

These considerations, as a rule, I do not mention at the time, but reserve them until the end of the examination, or such time as I may choose to make suggestions to the applicant in regard to his choice of occupation.

18 CHOOSING A VOCATION

I next question the applicant about his education, reading, etc.

What schooling have you had?

In what studies did you make the best records?

In what studies did you make the worst records?

What studies did you like the best?

What did you like the least?

What rank did you take, on the whole, in school or at college?

Did you do your very best with your studies, or was your time and interest largely taken up with other matters, athletics, social affairs, etc.?

What reading have you done on your own initiative not required in connection with school work? Books, magazines, newspapers?

What are your favorite books of all you have read?

What are your favorite authors?

Have you read any history? If so, what?

Economics?

Government?

How do you spend your spare time?

Tell me how you spent each evening of last week?

When you have a holiday, what do you do with it?

What is it that interests you most?

If you were at the World's Fair, what would most attract you? What would you go to see first?

What are your ambitions?

What man in history, or what living man, would you be like if you could choose?

Such questions tend to throw light on the aptitudes and interests of the applicant, and also on his weak points and diversions.

Next I question the youth in regard to his experience.

When did you first go to work? At what age?

What did you do first?

How did you get that work? Did the employer come after you, or did you get the work upon your own personal application, or through the efforts of your parents or friends?

COUNSELORS AND APPLICANTS 19

What pay did you get at the start?

How long did you stay?

Did you like the work?

Did it meet with the commendation of your employer or those in authority over you? Or did they find fault with you?

Why did you leave?

What pay were you getting at the end?

What work did you do next?

Repeating in regard to this second and all following experience all the questions asked in relation to the first work done, and any others which may be suggested by the circumstances of the case.

Have you saved your money and invested it? If so, how?

How do you spend your money?

Is there any one dependent upon you for support?

Do you smoke?

Do you drink?

By the time this course of questioning is finished the counselor is able, as a rule, to classify the applicant with a reasonable degree of accuracy. The applicants fall into two main classes: First, those having well-developed aptitudes and interests and a practical basis for a reasonable conclusion in respect to the choice of a vocation. Second, boys and girls with so little experience or manifestation of special aptitudes or interests that there is no basis yet for a wise decision. The latter are asked to read books and magazine articles about various occupations, and as they read to visit various industrial institutions, watch the men at work, talk with them, ask them how they like their work and their pay and if there is anything they do not like and what it is, if they would advise a young man to enter their line of work or not, and why. The boy is asked in some cases to try his hand at various occupations — farming, taking care of animals, carpentry, machinist's work, setting type, selling goods, etc. — to broaden and deepen his practical experience, and bring to light and develop any special capacities, aptitudes, interests, and abilities that may lie dormant in

20 CHOOSING A VOCATION

him or be readily acquired by him. After some weeks or months of such reading, investigation, and practical self-development, the applicant may come back and have another interview, when it may be possible to arrive at some definite conclusion as to what line of work it may be best for him to prepare himself for.

In dealing with the first class of applicants it is often possible to make quite definite suggestions even at the first interview, as will be seen by any one who will carefully study the records of actual cases printed in this volume.

With such applicants I generally ask at the close of the questioning above suggested: —

> If all the boys in Boston were gathered here together and a naturalist were classifying them as he would classify plants and animals, in what division would you belong?
>
> In what respects, if any, would you excel the mass of young men, and in what respects, if any, would you be inferior to most?
>
> Would the classifying scientist put you in the mechanical group or the professional group, the executive group or the laboring group?
>
> Would he class you as artistic, as intellectual, or physical, quick or slow, careful or careless, enthusiastic or unenthusiastic, effective or ineffective, etc.?

This focuses the attention of the young man on the characteristics that have been brought out during the interview, and helps him to place himself in the class where he belongs. Then we take the tables that show the conditions of success in different lines of industry, and go over them together in connection with what has been brought out in relation to the young man, to see if any valid conclusions can be drawn as to the true relations between the interests, aptitudes, and ambitions of the applicant and the advantages and disadvantages, and the conditions of success in different industries.

If the youth already has a good start or an excellent op-

COUNSELORS AND APPLICANTS 21

portunity in some line of work for which he is reasonably well qualified, the question may come whether it is not better for him to follow up this opportunity than to go off and try to build up a career in a new line which, though it may be somewhat more attractive to him, is far less easy of access and much less certain to produce successful results.

With both classes of applicants it is a common thing for the counselor, after a little questioning, to give the youth one of the Bureau's sheets of instructions, and a leaflet on personal investigation together with a standard blank book which we buy at the rate of one dollar a hundred, and ask the applicant to make a careful study of himself with the help of his friends, answering in the book so far as possible all the questions in the list, and then come back for another interview.

The case may be so clear that this is not necessary; but where the questions of the counselor do not bring out decided aptitudes and abilities or clear indications of wise policy in the choice of an occupation, this fuller study should be made by the applicant, and it is an excellent thing for him to make it in any case, though not by any means essential in all.

While I am questioning the applicant about his probable health, education, reading, experience, etc., I carefully observe the shape of his head, the relative development above, before, and behind the ears, his features and expression, color, vivacity, voice, manner, pose, general air of vitality, enthusiasm, etc.

The answers to the questions above suggested and the way in which the answers are given generally afford a good idea of the young man's mental development; his memory, reason, imagination are practically an open book to one who will question him carefully in detail for half or three quarters of an hour. And his business experience, the attitude of employers toward him and his attitude toward them, his

CHOOSING A VOCATION

reasons for leaving this, that, and the other place, all afford evidence of his disposition, efficiency, and general character.

But special tests may be applied wherever the counselor may deem it best. For instance, the memory may be tested by reading to the applicant from some book of good English sentences of 10, 15, 20, 30, 50 words, and asking the applicant to repeat the sentence read. He may also be asked to read himself and then repeat or write the sentences. If he can remember only 10 or 12 words correctly, his verbal memory is poor; if he can remember 40 or 50 words, it is pretty good. The readiness and certainty with which he can give dates and details in regard to his business experience and of his past life is in itself an excellent memory test.

Sometimes the counselor may wish to test the nerve and delicacy of touch. One way to do this is to have a series of very small circles a sixteenth or a thirty-second of an inch in diameter, and giving the applicant a fine-pointed pencil, ask him to put a dot precisely in the centre of each little circle and one exactly in the middle between each two circles, and make a certain mark at a given point on each of the circles in the group.

Rapidity can be judged by testing the swiftness of reading and writing and walking, and if a psychologic laboratory or some psychologic apparatus is available, it is easy to apply much more accurate tests through the phenomena of reaction-time, association-time, etc., than are readily available without scientific apparatus.

If the applicant's head is largely developed behind the ears, with big neck, low forehead, and small upper head, he is probably of an animal type, and if the other symptoms coincide he should be dealt with on that basis.

If the voice is harsh, or unpleasant, or lacking in vitality, I generally give the youth a lecture on the value of voice culture and the use of clear, sweet, well-modulated tones in conversation.

COUNSELORS AND APPLICANTS 23

If the face is blank and expressionless, a talk about the economic value of the smile is in order.

If the handshake is listless or wet, clammy or too forceful, it is well to call the young man's attention to his defects in this respect. So if the manners are in any way objectionable or undeveloped, the boy should be frankly but kindly told and urged to correct his errors.

In other words, the counselor should use the utmost frankness and kindliness in a friendly effort to enable the applicant to see himself exactly as others see him, and correct whatever defects may stand in the way of his advancement.

If the young man has not developed a proper interest in civic affairs, the counselor may try to quicken his development as a citizen by making suggestions in relation to books that he may read or organizations that he may join in order to bring out that side of his nature. If the young man has any bad habits, the counselor's questioning in relation to how he spends his spare time, how he spends his money, etc., is pretty apt to bring out the facts. And then it is the counselor's duty, in a mild and kindly but firm and energetic way, to make suggestions that will show the young man clearly the disadvantages of such habits and what will be the outcome if he persists in following them.

The counselor will find it greatly to his advantage if he will commit to memory the series of questions above suggested, or their equivalent, so that he can ask them readily without referring to any written or printed memoranda. The spontaneity of the examination is very important in securing the best results. The counselor should also familiarize himself with the specimen cases printed in this book, so that they may be to him what the leading questions in the law become to a first-class judge or lawyer. Every one of our leading questions should be firmly fixed in the memory, so that when a new case occurs analogous

CHOOSING A VOCATION

to one on record, the latter will immediately come to the mind of the counselor to aid him in classifying the applicant and making suggestions that may be most advantageous to him. No close adherence to precedent is urged, of course, but only so clear and thorough a grasp of our leading cases that they may be used to throw constant light on the new problems that arise. The counselor should also make a special effort to master and use the concrete form of suggestions. Instead of simply saying to the mistaken would-be doctor: "You would probably be at a great disadvantage in the pursuit of that profession," say to him, after bringing clearly to his mind the contrast between himself and the ideal doctor, something like this: *"Do you want to run a race with an iron ball tied around your leg, or would you rather enter a race where you can run free like the rest?"* So again, instead of saying to a youth: "You have got a pretty good start where you are; why not stay and develop that?" put the matter in some such form as this: *"You have a house half or two thirds built, the walls well up, almost ready to put the roof on; now is it wise to leave the building you have so nearly completed and go off to a new location, dig a new cellar and begin building all over again, when you do not know that you will like the new building any better than this one, after you get it?"*

This picture-method of presenting the case never fails to interest the youth, and often proves far more convincing than any form of direct statement that could be used.

The counselor should gather for himself all possible information in regard to the conditions of success in different lines of work and the distribution of demand in different industries, supplementing our tables by original research. He should also have full information in regard to courses of study, so that he can aid the applicant in choosing the best means of preparation for the calling he decides upon. The counselor will do well also to gather biographic data

COUNSELORS AND APPLICANTS 25

relating to the characteristics of leading men in their youth, and the relation between these youthful traits and the development of later life. If possible, a picture of the boy and of the man in his maturity should be secured to go with each one of these skeleton biographies. Such pictures and materials may be obtained in many cases from leading magazines and other publications, or may be had in response to direct communication with the men whose biographic data are wanted. Such skeleton biographies will be found of the greatest interest to young men and women who are trying to decide upon their life work, and will prove most useful to the counselor in making up his mind as to the classification of the applicant, his future possibilities, and the suggestions it may be best for the counselor to make to him.

IV

EXTENDED DISCUSSION OF PERSONAL DATA

As I have already said, no general rule can be given that will fit all cases. The method must be varied with the varying personal situations. A fifteen-minute interview will often bring the counselor to a definite opinion as to the advice to be given. In many cases, however, the problem is extremely difficult, and the counselor will wish to go into minute details with the applicant. For this purpose the following form is given at the risk of some repetition. The counselor can seldom take time to go into all this close analysis with the applicant, but the questions should be handed to the applicant, who can take them home and make them the basis of a thorough self-study.

To the applicant for vocational counsel: —

After you have written the answers to the following questions as far as you can, the counselor will meet you to discuss the record and any other questions the counselor may wish to ask, and to consider the problems of vocation, location, preparation, and development that you may desire to deal with, — what occupations you are best adapted to, the opportunities for employment in them, and the best means for the preparation and building up of a successful career.

The counselor will also aid you in coming to true conclusions on points of the schedule regarding which self-judgment may be difficult. But you should first do the best you can by self-examination, with such help as you may get from your family, friends, teachers, employers, and critics. Ask them to tell you what they think of you in relation to the various elements of manners, mind, character, etc., given below, and assure them that you want to know the truth, because you want to get acquainted with yourself.

DISCUSSION OF PERSONAL DATA   27

If you hide your limitations and defects from yourself, you may hinder your advancement quite as much as by neglecting your abilities and opportunities.

All the information and assistance we can give are freely at your service, but the more light you can bring to bear on the problem from your own observation, reading, and experience, the better it will be for the clearness and strength of the conclusions arrived at, and the permanent value of the results attained.

The first step is self-study. To *Know Thyself* is the fundamental requisite. Efficiency, success, and happiness depend very largely on adaptation to your work. You have therefore to investigate yourself, with the aid of the counselor and your friends, in order to determine your capacities, interests, resources, and limitations, so that you may compare yourself with the conditions of success in different industries.

Perfect truth and frankness with yourself and the counselor are absolutely essential to the best results.

Try to see yourself as others see you, and plan the future with a real knowledge of the nature, resources, and conditions you have to deal with, the purposes you may reasonably hope to accomplish, and the means by which you can move steadily toward the best success of which you are capable.

Write your answers on ordinary letter sheets 8x10. Use only one side of the paper. Number each answer to correspond with the question.

PERSONAL RECORD AND SELF-ANALYSIS.

PART I.

1. Name.
2. Address.
3. Where born and brought up.
4. Family you were born in; total number in it.
5. Ages of father and mother.
6. Nationality of father and mother.
7. Number and ages of brothers and sisters.
8. Business or occupation of father, brothers, uncles, and other near relatives.
9. Health of family; sickness record.
10. Do you live with the family?

CHOOSING A VOCATION

11. Ancestry — grandfathers, great-grandfathers, etc., nationality and residence.
12. Occupation and resources.
13. Physique, health, hereditary diseases.
14. Length of life.
15. Characteristics, special traits of body, mind, and character.
16. Your age.
17. Married or single. Your family if married.
18. Height and weight.
19. Health.
20. Sickness record.
21. How much time have you lost by sickness in the last five years?
22. Strength: What tests have you undergone?
    What hard work have you done?
    How much have you lifted?
25. Endurance: How far have you walked in one trip?
    Give distance and number of hours it took.
26. Courage: How have you acted when in danger, or suffering pain, disappointment, or loss?
27. Compare yourself as to strength, endurance, and courage, with others of your age, and with the best standards you know or have heard of.

State the facts with dates, as near as you can.

28. Habits as to fresh air, exercise, bathing, and diet.
29. Do you sleep with your windows open?
30. Do you breathe deeply in the fresh air every day?
31. How often do you bathe?
32. Have you studied physiology and hygiene?
33. Habits as to smoking.
34. Drinking.
35. Use of drugs.
36. Other forms of dissipation.
37. Education and training.
38. General education.
39. In school, what schools?
40. Best records in school, prizes.

DISCUSSION OF PERSONAL DATA 29

41.   Poorest records, in what?
42.   Out of school, by
43.   Reading, what, how, results.
44.   Favorite books.
45.   Favorite authors.
46.   Teaching ⎫
47.   Working ⎬ What have you learned by these means?
48.   Association ⎭
49.   Industrial education.
50   What courses and when?
51.   Manual skill, drawing, use of tools, etc.
52.   Sketches from memory (Consult with counselor about filling in this question).
53. Experience and present use of time.
54.   Positions held and work done, pay, and length of time in each case.
55.   Reasons for leaving in each case.
56.   Attitude towards employers — cordial and sympathetic, or not.
57.   Do you watch for the bell to ring and stop as soon as it stops?
        What are the prospects of rising where you are? Are you on friendly terms with your bosses? Have employers said anything in commendation or complaint?
58. Do you realize that wages depend largely on the efficiency and productive value of the workers?
59. Do you hope to be an employer yourself some day?
60. By what methods does advancement generally come, according to your observation?
61. Through what means do you hope to secure advancement?
62. Savings.
63. How do you spend your money?
        Why have n't you saved more of your money?
64. Most interesting or notable things in your life.
65. Likes and dislikes, pictures, music, theatre, books, dogs, horses, athletics, etc.
66. Favorite amusements.
67. How your evenings are spent.
68. How each evening last week was spent.

CHOOSING A VOCATION

69. Dominant (or ruling) motives and interests.
70. What do you look for first in the newspapers?
71. What would you buy and do next week if you had a million dollars left you?
72. Is there anything you would rather have than money?
73. If so, what?
74. On what occasions have you put forth your strongest efforts?
75. For what purposes?
76. If you were to visit a great international exhibition like that at St. Louis a few years ago, or the Centennial at Philadelphia, or the World's Fair at Chicago, where you could see splendid grounds and buildings, beautiful fountains and electric lighting effects, magnificent collections of manufactured goods, agricultural, dairy, forestry and mining products from all the leading countries, machinery, paintings and sculpture, educational and governmental exhibits, men and women of many nations, wild animals, military and naval displays, etc., etc., what would interest you most?

What would you want to see first?
What would claim your chief attention?
What would come second in attractiveness for you? Third? Fourth?
What would have least interest for you?

77. If you could travel wherever you wished, what countries or regions would you visit first?
78. Why? Give reasons for each of the countries or regions you specially wish to see.
79. Ambitions.
80. What would you be and do if you could?
81. If you had Aladdin's lamp and could have your every wish fulfilled, what would be your first half-dozen wishes?
82. Important things you have accomplished.
83. Distinguishing characteristics, aptitudes, capacities, abilities, and attainments.
84. Limitations and defects to be recognized.

If all the boys and girls in Boston were to meet to be compared with you, in what respects, if any, would you excel most of them, and in what would you be inferior to most?

DISCUSSION OF PERSONAL DATA   31

85. Compare your distinguishing abilities and limitations with the conditions of success in different callings, especially in those that lie in the direction of your ambition, as shown by the careers of men and women who have been successful in that line, and of those who have failed in it.

86. Have you studied the lives of Lincoln, Franklin, Garfield, Garrison, Phillips, Roosevelt, Gladstone, Wanamaker, Edison, and others, so as to discover as far as you can the laws of success, — why and how some men succeed, and what are the causes of failure?

87. Resources.

88.   Financial.

89.   Relatives.

90.   Friends.

91. Organizations you are connected with and how.

92. Organizing ability. Evidence. What organizations have you been instrumental in forming?

93. Describe briefly what you did, and the results.

94. Environment.

95.   What places have you lived in?

96.   If towns, or cities, give street and number in each case.

97.   Dates also, if possible, or your age, as nearly as you can, in each place.

98.   Describe the neighborhoods of each residence.

99.   Trees, grass, flowers, water, scenery?

100.   Class of people you were living among in each case.

101.   What did they work at?

102.   What were their amusements?

103.   What kind of life did they lead?

104.   Did you mingle with them freely?

105.   As one of them?

106.   If not, what were your relations with them and your attitude toward them?

107. Which, if any, of your residences were your own choice?

108.   Reasons for your choice in each case?

109. Who selected the other residences?

110.   Why?

111.   What sort of people do you prefer to live with now?

112.   Why?

CHOOSING A VOCATION

113. What effect do you think your locational environment has had on your ideals and ambitions, habits of thought and action, industrial opportunities and adaptability?

114. Would your opportunities and chances of success be greater in a smaller place, or in the country?

115. In the West or South?

116. In Europe, Africa, New Zealand, or Australia?

Give reasons for the opinions you express on these points.

DISCUSSION OF PERSONAL DATA   33

PART II.

The counselor will help you to reach correct conclusions on these points, but you should first make the best judgments you can by means of self-investigation and the help of your family, friends, teachers, employers, critics, — any one who will tell you what they really think about you. What they say may not be wholly right, — they may make mistakes, or they may be prejudiced in your favor or against you, — but their statements are valuable evidence to be considered by you in making up your mind what the truth really is.

Appearance, Manners, Conversation, etc.

Figure, slim, medium, thick-set, fat, plump, angular, straight, or crooked, bent, round - shouldered, hollow-chested, bow-legged, or otherwise defective.

Face, color, outline, features, symmetry, expression.

Hair, color, quantity, outline, adaptation to face and figure.

Dress, colors, fit, style, adaptation.

Do you give much attention to dress?

How long does it take you to dress?

How much do your clothes cost a year, including hats, shoes, neckties, underwear, and all apparel?

Do you take expert advice as to color, style, fit, etc.?

Neatness. Are your collars and cuffs Caucasian?

Are you careful to be clean and neat in dress and person?

Or do you wear your finger-nails in mourning and your linen overtime?

Postures, sitting and standing.

Are they refined, graceful, vigorous, or the contrary?

Look in the glass. Watch yourself. Get your friends to look you over in private and in public, and tell you confidentially what they think of your appearance, manners, voice, etc. You can do the same for them if they are willing.

Compare yourself in every detail with people you admire and with those you dislike, and study how to acquire the excellences of the former and avoid the faults of the latter. Get your family and friends to help you recognize your defects, and tell you every time you fail to come up to the standard you set for yourself.

CHOOSING A VOCATION

Do you stand straight or stooping?

Do you sit upright, chest out, or loll a limp heap in your chair?

Do you carry your chin forward, or your head tilted to one side?

Motions, rapid or slow, graceful or not, excessive or not.

Smile, frequent, rare, or absent, intermittent or perpetual, natural or forced, friendly or supercilious, frank or cordial, or cunning and unsympathetic, attractive or repellent.

Do you smile naturally and easily and feel the smile in your heart, or is your face ordinarily expressionless, or tinged with frowns, scowls, sneers, or in any way uninviting or repellent?

Do you realize the economic and social value of natural, friendly, cordial smiles, and of merry laughter, not so loud or frequent as to become annoying or monotonous?

Do you cultivate smiling as one of the winning graces that make life richer?

And do you cultivate smiles and laughter by right methods,— not mechanically but at the root, by cultivating the merry moods and friendly feelings that naturally express themselves in smiles?

Handshake, warm and cordial, or wet, clammy, listless, medium pressure, no pressure, or a vice-like grip that makes the individual regard you as a relic of the Inquisition, hasty, moderate, or long-drawn-out, quiet, or with one or two movements, or with pump-handle motions, more or less numerous and extensive.

Do you shake hands like a steam engine, or a stick, or an icicle, or like a cordial friend?

Have you cultivated a handshake that is warm and hearty, and yet not so strong as to be uncomfortable, nor so weak as to seem indifferent?

DISCUSSION OF PERSONAL DATA   35

Manners, in general, quiet, noisy, boisterous, deferential or self-assertive, listening politely or interrupting and contradicting. Careful of etiquette at table or not.

Are you thoughtful of the comfort of others?

Are you frank, kindly, cordial, respectful, courteous in word and actions?

Do you love people and show your friendliness in voice and manner?

Or do you feel and show indifference and dislike?

Do you look people frankly in the eye? Or do you avoid their gaze? If so ask yourself why.

Do you whistle or hum or make little noises with hands or feet, where others may be disturbed thereby?

Have you any habits little or big that may be disagreeable to others?

Voice, inflections. — Is your voice soft or loud, clear, smooth, musical, full of vitality; or rough, harsh, unmusical, clouded, husky, nasal, languid, gloomy, discouraged?

Are you careful about modulation, emphasis, and inflection?

Do you talk pretty much on one tone or a few tones, or do you watch the tones of speech that please you in others and the emphasis that gives form and color to spoken words, and adopt the best examples for your own use?

Are your inflections natural, cheery, courteous, respectful, modest, musical; or aggressive, discourteous, self-assertive conceited, affected, unmusical, pessimistic, repellent?

Have you cultivated your voice?

Do you take care to pronounce your words clearly and correctly?

Conversation. — Can you readily enter into conversation with new people?

Are you at ease with them?

Do you try to find out what they would like to talk about and make the conversation agreeable to them, or do you expect them to listen to the things that interest you?

Do you talk a good deal about yourself, your business, your ideas, your ailments, and other accomplishments, or mostly about public questions, or about the weather, the crops and the current scandals, murder trials, etc.?

CHOOSING A VOCATION

Are you a good listener, sympathetic, and really trying to get at the thought of your friend, or do you simply tolerate his talk and spend the time in thinking what you will say when he gets through?

Do you do most of the talking, or do you draw out your companions and listen to them most of the time?

Do you smile when they differ from you and quietly state the facts and reasons for your view, or say you think there is force in what they say and you will think it over; or do you show irritation at their stupidity in disagreeing with you, assert your conclusion and deny theirs with heat, and perhaps call them hard names or slur their intelligence?

Have you studied conversation as a fine art? Do you prepare for it, — look up or think up and fix freshly in mind some pleasant and interesting things to say when you meet people? You can put on some good ideas, as well as a good coat and a clean shirt, when you go out to spend the evening.

Personal atmosphere, cheery, animated, vivacious, full of good nature, or solemn, sleepy, indifferent, taciturn, morose.

Mind and sense, powers of attention, observation, memory, reason, imagination, inventiveness, thoughtfulness, receptiveness, quickness or stupidity, analytic power, constructiveness, breadth, grasp. Faculties specially developed. Faculties specially deficient. Form of head.

What tests have you undergone? In school and work and play, have you noted what powers you excel in and what you are deficient in, as compared with your companions? What light do your records in school and at work throw on the question?

Have you asked your family, friends, and teachers to help you locate your strong points and your weak ones?

Sight, normal, near or far, color sense, acute or medium, or color blindness.

Have you considered how much is due to capacity, and how much to training or the lack of it?

Hearing, normal, defective, or acute.

Smell, normal, defective, or acute.

Knowledge of self, motives, abilities, weaknesses, etc. of human nature.

State what means you have used to get a knowledge of these things.

DISCUSSION OF PERSONAL DATA   37

of business or industry.

of government.

of laws and causes.

of things, cities, countries, etc.

of language.

of law.

of medicine.

of science, physiology, hygiene, psychology, sociology, ethics, economics, physics, chemistry, metallurgy, mechanics, agriculture, horticulture, forestry, entomology, botany, zoölogy, biology, geology, astronomy, mathematics, arithmetic, algebra, geometry, analytic geometry, descriptive geometry, calculus, quaternions, surveying, engineering, architecture.

Mark the classes of books you are most familiar with, and the best books you have read in each class you mark.

Mark the sciences you have studied in school with an (S), if in college mark with a (C), and those you have read on your own account mark (R), and give the name of the book and author.

Of history and biography.

Of literature, fiction, philosophy, essays, humor, nature books, etc.

Skill. What ability have you to put your knowledge in action, to express your ideas through your body?

Skill of the hand.

What training and skill of hand have you in industry?

Do you draw, paint, or sculp?

Do you play any instrument? What?

Can you read or speak in public?

Public Speaking.

What have you done in this line?

Can you act or imitate others?

What have you done in this direction?

Singing.

Do you sing? What part, etc.?

Can you impart your knowledge? Can you teach?

Character.

Nothing is more vital than this. Health, ability, and character are the main factors in the best success. High character linked with ability — power and training of mind and body — can accomplish almost anything.

CHOOSING A VOCATION

In examining your characteristics and making up your mind what traits should be developed and what repressed or extinguished, there are some broad tests you can use to great advantage. Ask yourself the following questions, and act on the answers you get from your conscience and insight: —

(1) *"Would I like to have a strong novelist,* like Victor Hugo, Walter Scott, Thackeray, Howells, or the author of 'Sherlock Holmes,' *describe me just as I am,* — acts, words, thoughts, motives, turning the light on so the whole world would know the exact truth about me?"

(2) "What changes would I like to make in the picture?"

(3) "Can I not make those changes, or many of them, in the original?"

(4) "Am I the kind of man I wish my sister to associate with, become intimate with, and marry? If not, am I fit to associate with her and with my mother and other nice people?"

(5) "Am I the kind of man I'd like to see the world full of? If not, what improvements must I put on myself in order to win my own approval, and attain the type of manhood I would be willing to have increase and multiply and occupy the planet?"

You can test yourself in greater detail by putting a cross beneath each word that is in capitals, in the following list of characteristics, which seems to you fairly applicable to yourself.

If you judge yourself to come between the traits named, as if you think you are neither painstaking nor reckless, put your cross *mark on the line* between the two extremes.

Do not fail to read the side notes carefully, and act on their suggestions to the best of your ability.

HONEST	DISHONEST
TRUTHFUL	UNTRUTHFUL
CANDID	DECEITFUL
PROMPT	DILATORY
RELIABLE	UNRELIABLE
TRUSTWORTHY	UNTRUSTWORTHY

Do not place too much weight on your estimates of your own character, but do your best to form true judgments by looking at your acts and words and motives and judging them as you would if they were the acts, words, and motives of another person.

In weighing yourself on this count, ask yourself whether you do things that

DISCUSSION OF PERSONAL DATA   39

you would consider evidence of dishonesty or untrustworthiness if others did them; and whether, if you were an employer, you would trust a person who did or said these things with your money, property, or business.

State the facts on which your conclusions are based, especially the facts showing that you are or have been trusted or have proved yourself worthy of trust

JUST	UNJUST
SQUARE	UNFAIR
HONORABLE	DISHONORABLE
HIGHMINDED	LOWMINDED

Do you act in ways which when adopted by others you regard as taking unfair advantage, acting meanly or dishonorable for the sake of money or against justice and right, under the control of low motives or selfish interests?

CONSCIENTOUS	UNSCRUPULOUS
STANDING FOR	WILLING TO DO
THE RIGHT	AND SAY QUESTION-
REGARDLESS	ABLE THINGS FOR
OF CONSE-	MONEY OR POSITION
QUENCES	OR OTHER ADVAN-
	TAGES

Call to mind the specific facts.

When have you sacrificed advantage to right?

When have you sacrificed right to advantage?

CAREFUL	CARELESS
PAINSTAKING	RECKLESS
THOROUGH	SLIPSHOD
EFFICIENT	INEFFICIENT

After marking the words that seem to apply to you, submit the paper to friends who know you well, to see if they agree with your markings.

Or, better still, ask some of your best friends to mark other schedules to represent their estimates of you, and then compare notes.

If two or three of you work on separate papers at the same time, and then see where your markings differ and discuss the reasons frankly, you will get a great deal of light on your virtues and defects.

You can simplify the matter somewhat, perhaps, by writing all the good qualities in one long column, and all the undesirable characteristics in a parallel column; then putting a cross under each trait you think is yours, or two or more crosses if you have the trait very strongly developed.

You should revise your judgments from time to time with the aid of your friends, and note progress.

Make a list of the shortcomings it seems most important to eliminate as rapidly as possible, carry the list in your pocket, run over it every day, and note what you have done to get rid of the

40 CHOOSING A VOCATION

Do you do what you do the very best you possibly can?

Tendency to concentrate on one or a few things.	Tendency to spread attention and effort over a wide field. Many irons in the fire.
INDUSTRIOUS	IDLE
HARD-WORKING	SHIFTLESS
PERSISTENT	CHANGEFUL
STEADY	INTERMITTENT
ALERT	DULL OR ABSENT-MINDED
ATTENTIVE	INATTENTIVE
KEENLY ALIVE	APATHETIC
QUICK	SLOW
ACTIVE	PASSIVE
ENERGETIC	WORKING AT LOW PRESSURE
EARNEST	INDIFFERENT
ENTHUSIASTIC	WITHOUT ZEAL OR ENTHUSIASM
DEEPLY INTERESTED IN WHAT YOU ARE DOING	NO HEART INTEREST IN WORK. WORKING ONLY TO MAKE A LIVING.

State the facts on which you base your conclusions, and the reasons you manifest traits in the right-hand column if you conclude you have some of these traits.

SELF-RELIANT	TIMID, RETIRING
CONFIDENT	DISTRUSTFUL OR SELF
WILLING TO LEAD	INCLINED TO FOLLOW
ORDERLY	DISORDERLY OR INDIFFERENT
SYSTEMATIC, METHODICAL	NO ATTENTION TO METHOD, UNSYSTEMATIC

undesirable traits and form opposite habits.

New habits will be easily formed if you give constant attention and daily effort to the task.

For instance, suppose you are fighting untruthfulness, or carelessness, or bashfulness, or lack of thoughtfulness and smiling courtesy. Appoint some friend your confessor, and tell him or her every success and every failure, and in your struggles the successes will grow more and more numerous and the failures less frequent, and with earnest persistence the failures will vanish and you will have nothing but success to record.

Then you are ready to devote your attention to a new set of shortcomings, and so on until you have rounded out all the weak points in your character.

After a little you can impose a penalty on yourself also, if you choose, for every relapse. Human nature is plastic, and we can make ourselves good or bad, beautiful or ugly, admirable or disgusting, according to our will and effort.

DISCUSSION OF PERSONAL DATA 41

| HABITUALLY PLANNING AND WORKING BY WELL-CONSIDERED RULES | WORKING BY GUESS OR HABIT INSTEAD OF A DEFINITE PLAN |

Do you plan your work carefully as you would if you were going to build a house? Do you use system and scientific method in all you do?

| PROGRESSIVE | UNPROGRESSIVE |
| FULL OR INITIATIVE AND PUSH | NO INITIATIVE — SATISFIED TO GO ALONG IN THE OLD WAY |

Are you continually seeking new and better methods, and trying to improve yourself and your work?

OPEN-MINDED	BIGOTED
TOLERANT	INTOLERANT
WILLING TO LISTEN TO THOSE WHO DIFFER FROM YOU, AND TRY TO SEE THE STRENGTH OF THEIR FACTS AND REASONS	DOGMATIC, SURE YOU ARE RIGHT. TREATING THE IDEAS OF OTHERS WITH RIDI-CULE, SCORN, OR INDIFFER-ENCE, OR CLOSING THE MIND AGAINST THEM

How do you feel toward people of different creed, or political or economic faith? Do you welcome their thought and try to see if they have not caught some truth which has escaped you, or do you feel sure they are wrong, before you hear them, and either leave them alone with their error or talk with them only for the purpose of convincing them of their mistakes, or of showing apparent courtesy though really feeling no interest or welcome for their thought?

REASONABLE	UNREASONABLE
OPEN TO SUGGESTION AND CRITICISMS	SELF-OPINIONATED, OBDURATE
SENSIBLE	FOOLISH
PRACTICAL	IMPRACTICAL
SEEING THINGS IN TRUE LIGHT	FANCIFUL, DREAMY, UP IN THE AIR
WELL-BALANCED, POSSESSED OF "COMMON SENSE" AND "HORSE SENSE"	UNBALANCED, LACKING IN COM-MON SENSE, MAKING FRE-QUENT BLUNDERS, UNABLE TO MAKE THINGS COME OUT AS INTENDED

CHOOSING A VOCATION

WIDE-AWAKE	GREEN
SHREWD	EASILY IMPOSED ON
LONG-HEADED, FORESIGHTED	LACKING IN FORESIGHT AND SHREWDNESS

Think how often you have been imposed upon, and how often things have developed the way you thought they would, and how often not. On foresight is founded our control of the future.

KINDLY	CRUEL, HARSH, INDIFFERENT
SYMPATHETIC	UNSYMPATHETIC

Do you love animals, children, nature?
What pets have you had?
How did you make them do as you wished?
What kinds of people do you like?
What kinds do you dislike, and how do you treat them?
How do you act toward people who abuse you, or say mean things about you?
Ask yourself what you have done that might show kindliness and sympathy, and why you did these things.

HEARTY	COLD
CORDIAL	INDIFFERENT
AFFECTIONATE	UNAFFECTIONATE
LOVING	TENDENCY TO HATRED, DISLIKE, ANTAGONISM
DEMONSTRATIVE	UNDEMONSTRATIVE

Do you show your good-will and affection, or are you keeping them bottled up for use in some future epoch, or on another planet, or after the funerals of your relatives or friends?

RESPECTFUL	DISRESPECTFUL
COURTEOUS	DISCOURTEOUS
THOUGHTFUL OF OTHERS	BOORISH

Or negative in attitude toward others, neither courteous nor discourteous?

Tact. — Can you manage people well? State the evidence. Can you make people do as you wish by persuasion, or by leading them to adopt the suggestion as their own idea and act on it?
Do you make people feel comfortable and happy when you are with them?

DISCUSSION OF PERSONAL DATA   43

Do they seek your society and seem anxious to have you with them?

If not, what do you think is the reason?

Taste. — Do you know a fine picture when you see it?

Are you fond of pictures? Of music? What kinds?

Can you name some of your favorite pictures and pieces of music?

Can you tell an elegantly dressed person from one who is gaudily dressed?

Can you tell whether a lady's hair is becomingly put up or not?

Do you constantly ask yourself if your words and conduct are in good taste?

Temper.— Do you get angry easily?

What sort of things make you angry most quickly?

How many times have you been provoked during the last year?

What were the causes?

What did you do?

What fights or quarrels have you had in your life and why?

General disposition and make-up.

SELFISH	UNSELFISH
SOCIABLE	UNSOCIAL
TALKATIVE	TACITURN
WELL-SPOKEN	GOSSIPY
SELF-POSSESSED, CONFIDENT	SENSITIVE, EASILY EMBAR-RASSED
MODEST	VAIN AND EGOTISTIC, SELF-CONCEITED
BOLD	BASHFUL
COURAGEOUS	TIMID, SHRINKING, OR COW-ARDLY
GENEROUS	AVARICIOUS
FREE-HANDED	MISERLY
BENEVOLENT	CLOSE-FISTED
GOOD-NATURED, CHEERY	ILL-TEMPERED, SOUR, PEEVISH

44 CHOOSING A VOCATION

MIRTHFUL, MERRY, JOYOUS LIGHT-HEARTED	MELANCHOLY, MOROSE, FRETFUL, FAULT-FINDING, SARCASTIC, BITTER
CALM, SERENE	NERVOUS, EXCITABLE
SELF-POISED	EXPLOSIVE
DELIBERATE, acting on sober judgment after consultation and reflection	HASTY, IMPULSIVE
OPTIMISTIC	PESSIMISTIC
BUOYANT	GLOOMY, FOREBODING
HOPEFUL	DESPONDENT, DISCOURAGED
CONTENTED	DISSATISFIED, ENVIOUS
TENDENCY TO LOOK ON THE BRIGHT SIDE	TENDENCY TO LOOK ON THE DARK SIDE
A SPIRIT OF BROAD HUMANITY	NARROW, CLANNISH
QUIET	NOISY
GENTLE	STERN
REVERENT	IRREVERENT
DEMOCRATIC	AUTOCRATIC, SNOBBISH DESPOTIC
COÖPERATIVE	COMBATIVE, AGGRESSIVE
FINE AND STEADFAST IN FRIENDSHIP	UNRELIABLE, CHANGEABLE, TREACHEROUS
FRANK, CANDID, OPEN-HEARTED	SECRETIVE, CUNNING, UNDER-HANDED
TRUSTFUL, FORGIVING	JEALOUS, SUSPICIOUS

Will, weak, yielding, vacillating; or firm, strong, self-willed, stubborn?

Judgment.— Are you hasty and impulsive?

Or have you such mastery of yourself, such self-control, that you are able to act *contrary to present inclinations* for the sake of future benefit?

This is where foresight, judgment, and will-power unite to form one of the most vital and important elements of a strong character. To subordinate the present to the future and the lower nature to the higher, to form the habit of giving up a present pleasure for a greater future good, is one of the distinguishing marks of high type manhood and womanhood.

Purity in word, deed, thought.

DISCUSSION OF PERSONAL DATA   45

No answer is asked for here, for one who is impure cannot usually be trusted to tell the truth about it except to his own conscience. But he should never allow himself to forget that as long as he is impure he is living a tainted life, sacrificing his best to his lowest nature, and that there cannot be two standards; if he is acting or thinking in a way he would not wish his sister to think or act, he is not fit to look her or any other good woman in the eye or associate with her.

Temperance in food, drink, work, and amusement?

Humor. — Are you fond of humor?

> What humorous books have you read?
>
> Can you take a joke on yourself?
>
> Can you make a joke?
>
> Do you fix funny incidents and stories in your memory, and tell them to your friends?

Good fellowship.

Do you like to be with people?

And do they like to be with you?

Public spirit, patriotism, civic interest.

Are you a citizen?

If not, have you taken the proper steps to become one?

Do you always vote at primaries? At elections?

What means do you take to find out what men to vote for?

Do you read more than one paper?

Do you read any paper that is opposed to your party or political ideas?

What public questions are you specially interested in?

What have you done that shows your interest in public affairs?

Temperament. — Phlegmatic, buoyant, bilious, emotional.

Balance, or relative proportion of physical, mental, and emotional life and activities.

Reputation.

Ideals and theories of life and the world.

Friends.

How many intimate friends have you?

Describe the closest.

Are you planning to form further friendships?

> With what sort of people?
>
> By what means?
>
> For what ends?

46 CHOOSING A VOCATION

Personality. — Attractive or not, on the whole.

Have you observed why you are drawn to the men and women who attract you most? And examined to what degree you have the same qualities, and to what extent they are offset or nullified by unattractive or repellent qualities?

V

THE METHOD IN OUTLINE

IN brief outline the *Method* of the Vocation Counselor is as follows: —

I. Personal Data.

A careful statement, *on paper*, of the principal facts about the person, bringing out particularly every fact that has a bearing on the vocational problem.

II. Self-Analysis.

A self-examination, *on paper*, done in private, under instructions of the counselor, developing specially every tendency and interest that should affect the choice of a life work.

III. The Person's own Choice and Decision.

In a great majority of cases this will show itself in a marked degree before the work under I and II is finished. It must always be borne in mind that the choice of a vocation should be made by each person for himself rather than by any one else for him. The counselor can only guide, correct, advise, assist the candidate in making his own final choice.

IV. Counselor's Analysis.

On the basis of the information obtained under I and II, so far as possible the counselor should test III by making an analysis under each of the following heads, seeking in every line for significance in the line of the main quest: —

1. Heredity and circumstance.
2. Temperament and natural equipment.
3. Face and character.
4. Education and experience.
5. Dominant interests.

CHOOSING A VOCATION

V. Outlook on the Vocational Field.

One who would be a vocational counselor should familiarize himself in a high degree with industrial knowledge, and he will need some knowledge, as we have indicated in Part III of this book, that is not at present easily obtained. Investigations to be undertaken at once are:—

1. Lists and classifications of industries and vocations.
2. The conditions of success in the various vocations.
3. General information about industries, up-to-date, the kind that is found in current magazines and papers rather than in books.
4. Apprenticeship systems now in practice.
5. Vocational schools and courses available in your city and state.
6. Employment agencies and opportunities.

VI. Induction and Advice.

This calls for clear thinking, logical reasoning, a careful, painstaking weighing of all the evidence, a broad-minded attitude toward the whole problem, tact, sympathy, wisdom.

VII. General Helpfulness in Fitting into the Chosen Work.

PART II

THE INDUSTRIAL INVESTIGATION

VI

THE CONDITIONS OF EFFICIENCY AND SUCCESS IN DIFFERENT INDUSTRIES

Fundamental Requisites and Special Aptitudes, Abilities, Interests, Ambitions, and Traits of Character, in their Relations to Efficient Service and Industrial Success.

I. FUNDAMENTALS, applicable in large measure to all industries:

HEALTH	THOROUGHNESS	PROMPTNESS	RELIABILITY
INTEREST	ENTHUSIASM	SYSTEM	FORESIGHT
ENDURANCE	PERSISTENCE	COMMON SENSE	WILL POWER
ENERGY	HONESTY	MEMORY	JUDGMENT

Analytic method is an important factor, especially in intellectual pursuits, executive functions, and management.

A reasonable degree of *coöperativeness* is also essential to first-class success in nearly all lines of effort, and *love of the work* necessary to the best and fullest success.

It is true that in some rare cases, like those of Herbert Spencer and Alexander Pope, men may win success by the force of extraordinary genius in spite of ill health or physical disability. But such cases are very unusual, and for all ordinary cases it is substantially true that health is essential to success, and must be cultivated and safeguarded with the greatest care, as a fundamental requisite for bodily or mental achievement and the attainment of success and happiness. Knowledge of and obedience to the laws of health will pay bigger dividends than any other equal investment of time and effort.

It is also true that a certain appearance of success may be obtained without a full equipment of honesty. The burglar, the maker and vender of quack medicines and adulterated foods, the man engaged in the organized traffic for the manufacture of drunkards, the gambler, the commercial pirate who captures the wealth of others by means of railroad rebates or other unlawful advantages, the political pirate who corrupts our governments for plunder, — such men may secure the sham success, the pretense of prosperity that comes with the mere possession of money; but they cannot attain a real and lasting success, for that is beyond the reach of dishonesty. The burglar, the grafter, the commercial pirate, and their kind are in partnership with danger. Fear is their constant companion. The consciousness of evil and social disapproval and possible punishment poisons their lives. They are incapable of the free, full, abounding happiness that comes with a life of efficient service in harmony with social well-being. Even where the business of the pirate is partly or wholly within the law, as in case of the licensed saloon, there is no telling how soon the moral sense of the community may subject it to outlawry as well as ostracism. There is no true success, no success worth having, that rests on the dangerous and unstable basis of fraud and wrong. Even John D. Rockefeller, with all his millions, would have been a far happier man with an honest competence and the respect of his fellow men, than he can be now with the consciousness of the merited condemnation of all right-thinking people and the persistent hounding of the law that may at last bring him to justice for its violation, and compel him to pass his last days in ignominy and disgrace, if not in actual confinement. It is better to build a small house on the solid rock than to erect a palace on the quicksand.

II. The following particular conditions applicable to special industries or groups of industries are given, not as being comprehensive or necessarily accurate, but as illustrating the method applicable to any particular case. Some of these special conditions arise simply from the fact that full success in

CONDITIONS OF EFFICIENCY   51

the line indicated demands, in special amount or emphatic degree, one or more of the fundamentals.

(1) Agriculture, Horticulture, Floriculture, etc.
>Knowledge of soil, crops, processes, etc., best obtained by experience, linked with scientific study of the principles of the subject in a good school of agriculture, etc.
>
>Knowledge of the market and adaptation to it.
>
>Possession of a good area.
>
>A good degree of business capacity.

(2) Stock-raising, Dairying, and other Animal Industries.
>Knowledge of the life and habits of the animals to be dealt with.
>
>Sympathy with them and love for them.
>
>Knowledge of the market and adaptation to it.
>
>Capital, or management, or lease.
>
>A good degree of business capacity.

(3) Mining, Quarrying, etc.
>Prospecting:
>>Rugged health.
>>
>>Knowledge of geology, metallurgy, and chemistry.
>
>Operating:
>>Scientific knowledge of machinery and processes (or means to hire it).
>
>Knowledge of the market.
>
>Business ability.

(4) Mechanical Trades, Manufacturing and Construction, Transportation, etc.
>(a) Journeymen:

Skill of hand and eye.	Knowledge of the trade.
Care, accuracy, quickness, loyalty, hearty obedience to orders.	Ability to draw and to work by drawings,

>>Making employer's interest your own.
>>
>>Working as if the business were yours, or recognizing that in a very important sense it is yours as long as you are putting your life into it and depending on it for livelihood, promotion, and development.

CHOOSING A VOCATION

(b) Foremen, Superintendents, etc.:

Skill of hand and eye, and all essential qualities of journeymen.

Making employer's interest your own, etc.

Executive power, system.

Ability to get along with men and get the best out of them.

Knowledge of human nature.

Sympathy, appreciation.

Firm, kindly, tactful discipline.

(c) Owners, Managers, Heads of Departments:

All the qualifications of journeymen and foremen.

Organizing ability in proportion to the size and weight of the enterprise.

Knowledge of the market and adaptation to it.

Foresight, breadth and clearness of view.

The money sense.

Resources, inventiveness or ability to recognize and adopt new ideas of others.

Tireless planning and effort for improvement and development, to keep abreast of the times, and up to or ahead of competitors.

Location, capital, advertising, inventiveness, constructive, human, and artistic qualities of mind.

Inventiveness is very valuable throughout this group, but is not essential if the ability to recognize and adopt new ideas is persistent.

(5) Commerce: Wholesale and Retail, Buying and Selling.

(a) General sales force:

Knowledge of the goods.

Tact and skill in dealing with people.

Knowledge of human nature.

Care of stock and perfect knowledge of its location.

A spirit of genuine service.

Absolute reliability both in relations to employers and customers.

Attention, care, accuracy, quickness, enthusiasm, loyalty.

CONDITIONS OF EFFICIENCY 53

Extending to custom-
ers the courtesy,
consideration, and
helpfulness you
would desire in their
place.
Pleasant manners, cordial smile, etc.
Pleasant voice, well modulated.
Good conversational ability.
Attractive appearance, neatness, etc.
Good disposition, coöperative, good team-worker, patience, sympathy, good humor.

(b) Floor superintendents, foremen and forewomen, etc.
Knowledge of the goods, and all the accomplishments of salespeople in larger degree.
Executive ability.
System.

(c) Merchandise people, Buyers and Assistant Buyers, etc.
Knowledge of goods to a fine art.
Knowledge of market.
Judgment, foresight.
Energy, push, enterprise, resource, inventiveness.
Tact in dealing with people.

(d) Owners, Managers, Heads of Departments:

Skill of hand and eye.	Knowledge of the trade.
Care, accuracy, quickness, loyalty, hearty obedience to orders.	Ability to draw and to work by drawings.

Working as if the business was yours, etc.
Executive power, system.
Ability to get along with men and to get the best out of them.
Knowledge of human nature.
Sympathy, appreciation.
Firm, kindly, tactful discipline.
Organizing ability in proportion to the size and weight of the enterprise.

(6) Finance, Banking, Investment, etc.

(a) Cashiers, clerks, etc.:

Absolute reliability.	High character.

CHOOSING A VOCATION

Skill in special work.   Prompt, accurate, cheerful
service.

(b) Owners, managers, etc.:
Broad knowledge of business affairs.
Good judgment, caution.
Foresight.
Good business connections.
Reputation for sound judgment, square dealing, honesty, reliability, etc.
Ability to pick out the right men and get good results out of them.
Organizing and executive power.

(7) Agencies, office work, etc.
(a) General force:
Reliability, skill in special work.
Persuasive power, tact in dealing with people.
(b) Stenographic Force:
Technical skill, knowledge of English, care, accuracy, common sense.
(c) Managers:
Executive ability, organizing power, energy, push, enterprise, tact, coöperation.
Knowledge of the business.
Knowledge of human nature.
Ability to pick out the right men and get good results from them.

Throughout the Business Groups with which we have been dealing, executive power, organizing ability, system, energy, push, enterprise, inventiveness, resource, knowledge of business and markets, knowledge of human nature and tact in dealing with it, judgment, foresight, the money sense, are all very important factors in achieving the highest success and efficiency in the highest positions.

The contrast in the conditions of attaining high success in professional life and in business is very instructive.

The professional man, as a   The business man, as a rule,
rule,

CONDITIONS OF EFFICIENCY

1. Needs a great deal of *book knowledge.*
2. *Special* training in his business.
3. And must understand *people.*

But does not need organizing or executive ability in special measure, nor the money sense or financial judgment. Nor in most cases does he need either the coöperative spirit or competitive push in so high a degree as the business man

The professional man is an independent individual power.

Needs comparatively little *book knowledge.* Must know *things*, goods, markets, processes, etc. And must understand *people.*

He also needs organizing and executive ability in large measure, and the money sense or financial judgment. And the coöperative make-up as well as the push essential to aggressive competition.

The business man must build a big machine, including many human beings.

(8) The Professions.

(a) Teaching:

Love of the work, enthusiasm, sympathy with and interest in young people, character that commands respect, knowledge of the subject to be taught; knowledge of human nature; knowledge of method.

Health, endurance, patience, common sense, judgment, tact, good nature.

Memory, imagination, inventiveness, humor.

(b) Preaching and the Ministry:

Consecration to high ideals and standards of action.

Capacity for sacrificing the lower to the higher impulses and motives.

Admirable character.

Lovable personality.

Sympathy, deep, alive, active, expressing itself in deeds as well as words.

Common sense.

Power of expression.

CHOOSING A VOCATION

Knowledge of human nature and life, its joys and sorrows, hopes and fears.

Knowledge of ethical literature, history, government, industry, and science.

Memory, imagination, and humor.

Attractive appearance and address.

Pleasant voice, smile, handshake, etc.

(c) Authorship:

Vital knowledge of important subject or life experience.

Power of expression, skill in marshaling ideas in good order and attractive form.

Style, clearness, force, unity, inventiveness, sympathy, humor, earnestness, industry, knowledge of human nature, reputation, position, authority in reference to the subject, etc., location, friendship, etc.

Timeliness or adaptation to the age and interest of the people.

The *news sense*.

(d) Journalism:

Head line skill and inventiveness.

Power of expression, style, etc. (See Authorship.)

Common sense, good judgment, enterprise, push, assertiveness, knowledge of the community, politics, *business*, public men, history, etc.

Business Management.

(e) Medicine, Surgery, Dentistry:

Skill in diagnosis, which depends on knowledge of the body, symptoms, diseases, etc.

Powers of observation and analysis.

Constructive reasoning, or putting all the facts together to make a valid working hypothesis or rational conclusion on the whole case.

Skill in treatment, delicate adaptation to the individual case.

Caution, resource, knowledge of remedies.

Memory — volumes of facts.   *Nerve.*

Sympathy.   Eyesight.

Pleasing address.   Mechanical ability.

CONDITIONS OF EFFICIENCY   57

Attractive personality.   Inventiveness.
Fine *Character*.   Health.
                                   Love of the work.
Resources to buy a practice or live while building
   one.

(f) Engineering:
   High scientific ability, mathematical, mechanical,
      analytic, constructive.
   Years of special scientific training. Organizing power.
   Ability to manage men.

(g) Architecture:
   Constructive mind, inventive and adaptive power.
   Sense of harmony and proportion.
   Imagination and artistic bent.
   Knowledge of principles and history of architecture.
   Technical skill.
   Travel and visual acquaintance with best examples
      of architecture in various cities and countries.
   Wide culture, to develop power to express the best
      spirit of the time in architectural form.

(h) The Law:
   Understanding of human character and motives.
   Ability to deal with and influence men.
   Power of expression.
   Power of observation.
   Power of memory.
   Power of reason.
   Power of imagination.
   Common sense, clear thought, and forceful argument.
   Integrity, reliability.
   Humor, sympathy, kindliness, courtesy, combative-
      ness, persistence, indomitable will, resourcefulness,
      inventiveness, knowledge of law, knowledge of busi-
      ness and industry, knowledge of history, science, lit-
      erature, art.
   Location.
   Connections.
   Resources.
   Good appearance and address.

58 CHOOSING A VOCATION

(*i*) Statesmanship:

All the requirements for success in the law.

A knowledge of statecraft, diplomacy, political history and machinery, public men, public questions, the principal movements of the time, and interstate and international relations, etc.

Knowledge of men.

Memory for names and faces.

Organizing and executive power.

Constructive mind.

Coöperative make-up.

Organizing and directing ability of the highest type.

Commanding character and attainments.

Tact, courtesy, attractive personality.

(9) Semi-Professional Work:

(*a*) Politics, Legislature, Council, Elective Office.

Distinguished service or ability.

Identification with wealth or representative of a popular cause.

Influential friends.

Oratorical power.

Interest in public affairs.

Effective pushing of some important movement.

Readiness to render small services.

Good fellowship.

Memory of names and faces.

Wide acquaintance.

Common sense.

Humor.

Attractive personality.

Fine appearance and address.

(*b*) Lecturing, public platform work.

Personality. — Distinguished service, fame, person people wish to see and hear on account of what he has done.

Popular cause or movement. — Vital knowledge of important subject. Attractive method of presentation.

Style. — Simple, clear, forceful, rapid movement,

CONDITIONS OF EFFICIENCY 59

humor, appeal to the ideas and emotions of the average mind of the audiences.

Oratory. — Oratorical power, voice modulation, times of speech, vitality, earnestness, use of pause, gesture, facial expression, etc.

Novelty — advertising.

(c) Secretarial work:

Skill in correspondence.

Reliability, courtesy.

Care, accuracy.

Trustworthiness.

Knowledge of analytic method and research.

Knowledge of business, economics, public questions, etc., is also necessary in many cases, especially in employment by associations, corporations, trade unions, civic organizations, or leading men of affairs.

Organizing ability is frequently called for.

Tact, energy, push, and common sense.

(10) Artistic employments:

(a) Illustrating:

Technical skill.

Imagination.

Wide culture to give understanding and wealth of material.

Common sense and judgment in choice of subject.

Appreciation of reader's standpoint.

(b) Cartoon work:

Technical skill and training.

Knowledge of political affairs and current events.

Imagination.

Inventiveness.

Humor.

(c) Engraving:

Long and untiring practice.

Delicacy of touch, with firmness and certainty.

Extraordinary skill of hand and eye.

Perfection of nerve tone and control.

(d) Photography:

Ability to choose the best pose.

CHOOSING A VOCATION

Tact to get the "patient" in good humor, and bring out the best expression.

Skill to squeeze the bulb at the psychologic moment.

Artistic sense of form proportion, light and shade.

Technique.

Courtesy.

(e) Painting:

Artistic temperament, passion for form and color.

Color sense, form proportion.

Ability to choose an *artistic subject*, a subject worthy of the skill of an artist.

Knowledge of composition.

Technical skill with the brush.

(f) Sculpture:

Form, idealism, technique.

Artistic temperament, passion for form and its expression.

Fine sense of form and proportion.

Power to symbolize life, motion, and emotion in form.

Mastery of technique.

(g) Landscape gardening:

Sense of form and color and proportion.

Ability to make pictures on a large scale, not on canvas, with real trees and grass, buildings, fountains, lakes, and sky.

Artistic sense, and a brain full of images of beautiful scenes.

Imagination, technique, experience.

(h) Music:

Vocal:

Artistic temperament, natural gifts, musical memory.

Persistent culture.

Modulation and expression.

Good appearance.

Instrumental:

Artistic temperament.

Natural gifts — musical memory.

CONDITIONS OF EFFICIENCY   61

Persistent culture.
Modulation of expression.
Good appearance.
Manual skill.
Composition:
Artistic temperament.
Natural gifts.
Musical memory.
Inventiveness.
Imagination.
Ability by natural training to express emotion in harmonious combination of sound.
Study of best music, methods of composition, etc.

(i) Acting:
The artistic temperament.
Emotional nature, and a passion for expression by voice and movement.
Naturalness, repose, control, ability to express without over-expression, or excitement that tears the passion to tatters.
Memory, confidence, tireless industry.
Health and strength to stand the tremendous strain of rehearsals and continuous performances.
Fine appearance.
Opportunity.

(j) Elocution:
Training and technique.
Good voice, musical, full of life, well trained.
Judgment in choice of selections interesting to audience.
Modulation, expression, sympathy, personal power.
Attractive appearance and personality.

(11) Public service:
Post Office — Memory, geography, ability to decipher handwriting.
Police — Courage, strength, knowledge of human nature.
Fire Department — Quickness, fearlessness, agility, etc.
Army and Navy — Physical tests, obedience, etc.
Government Clerks — Accuracy, mathematics, special training.

62 CHOOSING A VOCATION

Consular Service — Languages, law, love of travel, etc.

Diplomacy, Ambassadors, etc. — Legal training, languages, etc.

(12) Social Work:

Love of the service, enthusiasm, character commanding respect.

Power of expression.

Organizing ability.

Understanding of the people among whom the work is to be done.

Knowledge of human nature in general.

Knowledge of society, government, industry.

Sympathy, tact, humor, coöperation.

Patience, kindliness, high ideals.

Good general education.

Special training in social problems, organizations, research, etc.

Attractive personality.

EFFICIENCY RECORDS

Employers of labor are becoming more scientific in their methods of judging the people who work for them. Snap judgments and guesswork are becoming a thing of the past. As indicating this tendency, I have secured permission to present here in part the schedules used in a certain large department store. There are three sets of record forms: one for executives, one for salespeople, and one for all other positions. The record for executives is varied by specific tests for the different classes of executives. Its general terms are as follows: —

NAME

I. PERSONAL DATA
    Date Entered   Positions Held
    Previous Experience
    Education

II. GENERAL REQUIREMENTS Merits Date Date Date Date Date Date Date
    Rating by the Manager

	Merits
Character	100
Health	100
Intelligence	100
Capacity for Learning	100

Every employee must stand at not less than 75% in each of these points.

A health rating of 50%, if temporary, may be allowed.

CONDITIONS OF EFFICIENCY

III. RESULTS
Rating by Head of Department

In Work	Merits	Date	Date	Date	Date	Date	Date
Work Well Organized	24						
Work Done Promptly	24						
Work Done Thoroughly	24						
Proper Control of Expense	24						

In Handling Employees	Merits	Date	Date	Date	Date	Date	Date
Satisfactory Results from Subor-dinates	24						
Satisfactory Relations with Subordi-nates	24						
Subordinates Developing Efficiency	24						
Training an Understudy	24						

In Executive Qualities

Initiative
Doing it without being told to. Jumping over red tape for results. Going ahead without waiting for the other fellow.   20

Responsibility
Faithfulness, regularity, punctuality, accuracy, balanced, safe judgment.   20

Concentration
Getting the thing done. No side tracks. Sticking to it. Capacity for work. Persistence. Will Power. Does he hit the nail on the head until it is driven.   20

Progressiveness
Is he growing? Does he study? Open-minded? Is he devoted to things as they are or to things as they ought to be?   20

Knowledge
Broad acquaintance among people. Human nature. His job. Our system. Other stores. Successful men and methods. Books.   <u>20</u>

Total

No rating carrying less than 200 merits is passable. Temporary allowance may be made for merits under IV.

IV. OUTLOOK FOR FUTURE RESULTS
Merits assigned by Superintendent

Studies	24
Personal Sacrifices for Success	24
Temporary Handicaps	48
Intelligent Ambition	10
Sane Enthusiasm	10
Courage	10
Energy	10
Suggestions	5
Helpfulness to others	<u>5</u>

Total

The limit of merits allowable to each item is indicated in first column.

64 CHOOSING A VOCATION

Rating marks indicate as follows: —

A (best) 100%; B (good) 75%; C (medium) 50%; D (poor) 25%; E 0%.

Percentage ratings may be used to indicate finer distinctions.

The record for salespeople in addition to I and II above, is as follows : —

III. SPECIAL QUALIFICATIONS	Merits	Date	Date	Date	Date	Date
Rating by Superintendent						
Salesmanship Training	100					
Manners	100					
Voice	100					
Physique	100					
Dress	100					
English	100					
Speed	100					
Accuracy	100					
Energy	100					
Taste (Buyer)	100					
Love for the Work	100					
Capacity for Work	<u>100</u>					
Average						

Every salesperson must have an average of at least 50% in Special Qualifications.

IV. RESULTS		
Rating by Floor Manager		
Filling Quotas	20	
Average Rating	20	
Service to Customers	16	
Selling Profitable Merchandise	12	
Merchandise Calls	10	
Travelers	4	
Stock Keeper	8	
Stock Display (Buyer)	4	
Punctual	2	
Regular	2	
Cheerful Compliance with Orders	<u>2</u>	
Total		

No rating of less than 75% in Results is passable, unless offset by III or V. All over 75% average under III, and all merits under V, may be temporarily added to the total under IV.

V. OUTLOOK FOR FUTURE RESULTS	
Merits assigned by Head Floor Manager	
Studies	5
Personal Sacrifices for Success	5
Temporary Handicaps	10
Questions about Goods	5
Sales Class Work	5
Suggestions	3
Helpfulness to Others	3
Executive Qualities	<u>10</u>
	100
Total	

The limit of Merits allowable to each item is shown in first column.

The record for persons in non-executive and non-selling positions is similar in general terms to the foregoing, and is varied for the different positions according to the judgment of the superintendent.

VII

CLASSIFICATIONS OF INDUSTRIES

EACH vocational counselor should make a thorough and detailed classification of the vocations. As no such list of vocations can be permanent, and as any list will probably be incomplete, I shall not attempt to present one here. On broad lines I would group the different industrial pursuits as follows: —

1. Agencies and Office Work.
2. Agricultural.
3. Artistic.
4. Commercial.
5. Domestic and Personal Service.
6. Fishing.
7. Manufacturing.
8. Mechanical, Building, and Construction.
9. Professional and Semi-professional.
10. Transportation.
11. Miscellaneous Industries.

One of the first tasks for a vocational counselor is the making of as complete a list under each one of these headings as possible.

One of the most serious limitations under which young people unconsciously live is their lack of an outlook upon the industrial world. It is of first importance that the applicant should know as much about the various fields of industrial pursuit as possible, and the first step is that he be given a comprehensive view of the field itself.

VIII

INDUSTRIES OPEN TO WOMEN

FOLLOWING is a list of women's ways of earning money, at home and away from home, indoors and out of doors, skilled and unskilled. It is not exhaustive, and is given here for its suggestive value only.

Plant Culture

Growing flowers — floriculture
    "   fruits
    "   plants, vines, etc., to
            sell
    "   trees — horticulture
    "   vegetables — market-
            gardening
    "   mushrooms
    "   seeds, bulbs, etc., for
            market
Tending other peoples' flowers
  at home or at their homes —
  flower doctor
Collecting flowers, making
  herbariums, etc.

Animals

Raising chickens, eggs, etc.
Keeping bees and selling honey
    "   silk worms
Dairy work

Raising cows
    "   horses
    "   sheep
    "   dogs
    "   cats
    "   rabbits
    "   birds

The better they are bred, etc., the more they are trained, the higher the price they will sell for.

Caring for other peoples' animals, — pet cats, dogs, etc
Collecting butterflies to sell
Care, training, and exhibition
  of *wild* animals.

Food Products

Putting up fruits, jellies, pickles,
  etc.
Making butter, cheese, etc.
    "   bread, pies, cakes
    "   candies, popcorn
Preparing stuffed prunes
    "   salted almonds
    "   seeded raisins

Textile Work

Plain sewing

Mending — darning for laundries, etc.
Making buttonholes
    "   clothing for stores and
            factories
    "   aprons, neckwear,

INDUSTRIES OPEN TO WOMEN

Cooking and selling meats
in slices or sand-
wiches, etc.
"   vegetables, etc., ready
for the table
Putting up box lunches to sell
to passengers on trains
or for clerks and work-
ers in stores and facto-
ries
Getting up light lunches for
parties
Catering for clubs, etc.

Board and Lodging
Keeping boarders
Renting rooms

*Miscellaneous Home Manufac-
tures*
Making tops
"   pincushions
"   baskets
"   leather goods
"   chairs
"   picture frames
"   perfumery
Artificial flowers
Bead ornaments, purses, etc.
Boxes
Belts, etc.
Upholstery

Domestic Service
Cooks
Waitresses
Chambermaids
Laundry girls
All-round servants
Housekeepers
Companions

wash rags, laundry
bags, show bags, etc.
Making infant booties, sacques
and underwear
"   tidies and sofa cushions
"   patchwork quilts
"   rag carpets, rugs, etc.
"   rag dolls
"   cloth animals, Teddy
bears, elephants,
dogs, etc.
"   Battenberg doilies and
centrepieces
Knitted and crocheted slippers,
shawls, scarfs, mittens,
wristlets, heavy socks, etc.
Lace - making, handkerchiefs,
etc.
Embroidery, collars, cuffs, etc.
Making tapestries
Dressmaking
Millinery

Store Work
Salesgirls
Bundlegirls
Cash girls
Bookkeepers, and other office
girls
Serving girls, repairers, etc.
Models, guides, etc.
Floor Superintendents
Window dressers
Stock Girls
Buyers and assistants
Managers
Welfare work

Factory and Shop Work
Shoe factories
Cotton and woolen mills

CHOOSING A VOCATION

Hotel and Restaurant
Cooks
Waitresses
Chambermaids
Laundry girls
Office girls
"The pleasant boarder"
Housekeepers

General Work
Washing and ironing
Scrubbing
Dusting carpets
House cleaning

Independent Commercial Callings, etc.
Storekeeping
Running employment office
    "   typewriting office
Dressmaking
Millinery
Hairdressing
Chiropody
Manicuring
Massage
Cleaning gloves, ribbons, etc.
Keeping clothing or apartments
    in order for bachelors, or fami-
    lies who wish such service
Packing trunks for guests at
    hotels, etc.
Emergency maid
Chaperoning
"Children's Club" work —
    playing with little children to
    relieve their mothers some
    hours a day
Matrons of Homes and Institu-
    tions

Box factories
Canning   "
Clothing   "
Laundries
Typesetting
Printing
Proofreading
Bookbinding
Etc., etc.

Office Work
Stenography and typewriting
Bookkeeping
Telegraphy
Telephone service

Agencies, etc.
Selling books — Canvassing
    "   bonds and stocks
    "   goods on commission
Demonstrating
Advertising
Life Insurance
Real estate
Officers of trade unions and
    other organizations having
    paid officials

INDUSTRIES OPEN TO WOMEN 69

Professional and Semi-Professional

Teaching in general
  Kindergartens
  Governess
  Public Schools
  Academies
  Colleges
  Special

    Music { Vocal / Instrumental

  Dancing
  Calisthenics

  Means of health and beauty { in gymnasium clubs / or private classes

  Teaching by correspondence
Authorship — Writing books, magazine articles, etc., science, art, poetry, fiction
Journalism — Writing stories, etc., for newspapers
Writing Advertisements
Interpreting
Translating
Lecturing

Elocution
Drawing
Painting
Sloyd
Modeling
Sculpture
Domestic Science
Dressmaking
Plain sewing and fancy
Millinery
Cooking teacher
Salesmanship teacher
Etc., etc.

Ministry
Mission Service
Medicine
Nursing
Dentistry
Law
Library work
Private Secretaryship
Traveler's guide
Manager or Director of gymnasium or other institution
Reading, singing, acting, etc. (see next division)

Artistic Occupations

Illustrating
Drawing patterns for embroidery, etc.

Photography
Retouching negatives
Coloring photos

Making designs for tiles, wall papers, carpets, etc.

Painting china

Landscape work

Portraiture

Arranging flowers for entertainments

Window decorating

Singing
Whistling
Dancing
Acting

In concert Theatre, or Private Entertainment.

Acrobatic exhibitions

Posing

Civil Service

Post office

Customs house

Factory inspection

Government clerks, etc.

Enlarging photos in crayon, India ink, etc.

Making articles of carved wood or burned wood, etc.

Sculpture

Architecture

House decorating

Landscape gardening

Beauty culture

Conducting orchestra

Playing the piano, violin, and other musical instruments

Exhibitions of magic

Social Work

In College settlements

" Charity organizations, etc.

Club work

Class work

Investigation, education, visitation — ministering to the civic and social life and economic development of the less fortunate, and enlightening, educating, organizing, and assisting the more fortunate in respect to their relations to the first group

Welfare work (see also store work)

Organizing coöperative enterprises and associations for mutual help, and civic and social betterment.

IX

THE USE OF STATISTICS

THE vocational counselor should be a careful student of industrial history and industrial geography. He should know how not merely to get the statistics, but how to use them. We have prepared and found useful a number of schedules throwing light on our problems in Massachusetts.

1. A list of the workers in the different industries per thousand of population (ten years of age, and over), in the chief cities of Massachusetts in 1900. (Information can be obtained from the special report on occupations, Twelfth Census, Table 42, page 428, etc.)
2. Capital invested in the various industries in Massachusetts, showing the number of establishments, number of workers, capital per employee, salaries paid managers and high officials, etc. (Information from U. S. Census, 1905, Manufactures, Part II, Table XIX; and 1902, Mines and Quarries, page 234, etc.)
3. Table on earnings, also taken from the United States Census Report, shows for each industry the total amount of wages paid, the average number of workers, and the average paid by the day.
4. Table showing the sex, color, and nativity of persons engaged in various occupations in the ten largest cities of Massachusetts.
5. Table showing the movement of demand from 1860 to 1900 in each of 199 vocations.
6. Table showing the movement of demand for females, giving the number of females engaged in different industries in 1870, 1880, and 1900.
7. Table showing the death rate per thousand workers in 150 occupations in Massachusetts.

72 CHOOSING A VOCATION

A few of the facts brought out in these tables may be of interest. For instance, the increase in the number of persons engaged in agencies and office work has been fifty per cent since 1860, while the population has only a little more than doubled itself, and there are thirty-two times as many women thus occupied as there were in 1870. At present there are twice as many men as women thus engaged.

In agriculture the figures of 1900 show a decrease of over one thousand persons since 1860. There were, however, ten times as many women in this work in 1900 as in 1870.

In domestic and personal service there were three times as many people employed in 1900 as in 1870, with only twice as many women.

The proportion of persons engaged in fishing remains about the same. The 1900 Census gives forty-four women so engaged.

In manufacture of food products, the proportion of workers increases slightly over the increase in population. The number of women engaged in this industry increased twenty times in thirty years, although men still greatly outnumber women in this field.

In the leather and shoe group of industries the proportionate number of workers has not kept up with the increase in population.

The operatives engaged in the different textile factories were not half as many more in 1900 as in 1870, although the population has almost doubled itself in that time. Even the number of women in this industry did not keep pace proportionately with the population.

In the professional and semi-professional group there were about five times as many persons in 1900 as in 1860. And here again women have increased their numbers in the largest ratio.

Turning to the question of earnings, we find that on the

THE USE OF STATISTICS 73

average in manufactures the highest wages are paid to those who are in the trades in which the trade unions have been most active.

Malt and distilled liquor workers average	$2.90 a day.	
Tobacco workers	"	2.10 "
Printers and bookbinders	"	2.12 "

The lowest earnings are to be found in

Confectionary trades	$1.04 a day.
Broom and brush-makers	1.07 "
Paper-box makers	1.16 "
Knitting mill operatives	1.16 "
Silk mill operatives	1.18 "
Cotton goods operatives	1.22 "

Coming to the question of salaries, we find the highest average salaries also in the

Malt and Distilled liquor business	$1933.33
Paper and paper goods.	1777.46
Chemical workers	1771.39
Cotton goods.	1767.70
Worsted mills	1770.70

The United States Census of 1900 does not state the earnings in many of the fields of industrial life. The practice of the various state statistical bureaus varies in this regard. If the vocational counselor cannot find the information that he wants from any of these sources, he can easily get a basis for a safe induction by selecting a group of individuals in any industry and getting his facts from them.

X

THE MOVEMENT OF THE DEMAND FOR WORKERS IN THE DIFFERENT INDUSTRIES

(UNITED STATES, 1870-1900[1])

IN considering the movement of demand, two things are of importance. First, by finding the increase or decrease in number of persons gainfully employed during the past ten, twenty, thirty, or fifty years, to discover the increase or decrease in the demand for workers in the different occupations during that time. Second, by reckoning the increase in proportion to population, to find whether this demand has grown with the population or fallen behind it.

To illustrate, the following table has been prepared. This shows that though the number of persons employed in agriculture has almost doubled since 1870, the number in proportion to population (the number per thousand) is less now than then; while all the other classes have grown, not only in actual numbers, but also in proportion to the total population.

General figures such as these, however, are of less value to one choosing a vocation than figures relating to specific occupations. We find, from the table given, that in 1900 about sixteen out of every thousand persons in the United States were engaged in Professional Service, while only about twelve in every thousand were thus engaged in 1870. But of more practical value is the knowledge of the details of the movement of demand, such as the fact that

---

[1] The figures given in the following pages for the United States apply to "Continental United States only." The figures given for 1870, 1880, 1890, and 1900 include all persons ten years of age and over.

TABLE I

Number of Persons Engaged in Each Main Class of Gainful Occupations per Thousand of Population (United States.)[1]

	1900		1890		1880		1870	
	ACTUAL NO. ENGAGED	NO. PER 1000	ACTUAL NO. ENGAGED	NO. PER 1000	ACTUAL NO. ENGAGED	NO. PER 1000	ACTUAL NO. ENGAGED	NO. PER 1000
All Occupations	29,073,233	381.02	23,318,183	372.36	17,392,099	346.76	12,505,923	324.33
Agriculture	10,381,765	136.06	9,148,448	146.08	7,713,875	153.8	5,948,561	154.27
Professional Service	1,258,538	16.5	944,333	15.08	603,202	12.02	371,650	9.64
Domestic and Personal Service	5,580,657	73.14	4,220,812	67.4	3,418,793	68.16	2,263,564	58.7
Trade and Transportation	4,766,964	62.47	3,326,122	53.11	1,871,503	37.31	1,244,383	32.27
Manufacturing and Mechanical Pursuits	7,085,309	92.85	5,678,468	90.67	3,784,726	75.46	7,085,309	92.86
1. Manufacturing and Mechanical Pursuits Proper	6,435,608	84.34	5,231,058	83.53	3,493,977	69.66	——	——
2. Mining and Quarrying	580,761	7.61	387,248	6.18	249,397	4.97	——	——
3. Fishing	68,940	.90	60,162	.96	41,352	.82	——	——

[1] The figures here given are for Continental United States. The occupation figures apply to all persons ten years of age and over, the population figures to the total population.

The sources for this table are the U. S. Census, 1900, volume on Occupations, Tables XXII, XXIX, IV; volume on Population, Part I, Table VII.

CHOOSING A VOCATION

between 1870 and 1900 the number of dentists increased almost fourfold, the number of "engineers (civil, etc.) and surveyors" and the number of journalists almost sixfold, the number of literary and scientific persons tenfold, while the demand for physicians and surgeons, lawyers and clergymen, though it had doubled during that time, varied little in proportion to the growth of population.

Often a general class of occupations will grow greatly while certain occupations included under it decline, or the reverse may occur. Thus Trade and Transportation has grown more rapidly than any other class, employing in 1900 sixty-two out of every thousand persons, whereas in 1870 it employed but thirty-seven. The number of boatmen and sailors, however, under Trade and Transportation has fallen from 105,072 in 1850 to 78,406 in 1900.[1] On the other hand, though Agriculture employed eighteen less per thousand in 1900 than in 1870, the number of stock raisers, herders and drovers (included under it) increased from 15,359 in 1870 to 84,988 in 1900, showing an increase of threefold in proportion to population.

One of the most interesting features in the growth of industries is the increasing number of women employed. In 1850 no women were entered in the occupation returns of the United States Census. In 1870, 1,836,288 out of 12,505,923 persons, and in 1900, 5,319,397 out of the 29,073,233 persons gainfully employed, were women.

Some occupations in which there an increase in the per cent of women employed and a corresponding decrease in the per cent of men employed are as follows: —

The percentage of women teachers to the total number of teachers rose from 67.6 in 1880 to 73.3 in 1900.

The percentage of women "musicians and teachers of music" rose from 43 in 1880 to 56.4 in 1900.

---

[1] This fact becomes more significant when we discover that in 1850 only free males, fifteen years of age and over, were included in the occupation returns, while in 1870, 1880, 1890, and 1900 all persons ten years of age and over were included.

DEMAND FOR WORKERS   77

The percentage of women employed as government officials from 3.1 in 1880 to 9.4 in 1900.

The percentage of women "artists and teachers of art" from 22.5 to 43.8.

The percentage of women employed in "literary and scientific pursuits" from 11.9 to 31.8.

The only occupation in 1900 in the professional class in which there was not an increase in the per cent of women employed, was that of "actors, professional showmen, etc.," in which the increase in the per cent of men employed was from 72.5 in 1880 to 79.1 in 1900.

"In the cases of architects, clergymen, dentists, lawyers, and physicians and surgeons, the percentages of women in 1900 were small, but showed a marked advance as compared with the 1880 percentages."[1]

For further changes in the per cent of men and women employed in the different occupations, see the United States Census for 1900, volume on Occupations, Table XLVIII and pages cxxxvii to cxxxix.

Two tables are appended to this chapter; one (Table II) giving the twenty occupations which in 1900 employed the greatest number of persons of both sexes, the twenty occupations employing the greatest number of men, and the twenty employing the greatest number of women. The other table (Table III) gives the occupations in which the total number of persons has increased most, and the occupations in which the number of women employed has increased most.

[1] See United States Census, 1900, volume on Occupations, p. cxxxvii.

TABLE II[1]

Occupations in which the Greatest Number of Persons are Employed, for Both Sexes and for Women separately, 1900.

DISTRIBUTION OF BOTH SEXES		DISTRIBUTION OF MEN		DISTRIBUTION OF WOMEN	
OCCUPATIONS	TOTAL NO. EMPLOYED	OCCUPATIONS	NO MEN EMPLOYED	OCCUPATIONS	NO. OF WOMEN EMPLOYED
Farmers, Planters, and Overseers	5,674,875	Farmers, Planters, and Overseers	5,367,169	Servants and Waiters	1,283,763
Agricultural Laborers	4,410,877	Agricultural Laborers	3,747,668	Agricultural Laborers	663,209
Laborers (not specified)	2,629,262	Laborers (not specified)	2,505,287	Dressmakers, Milliners, etc.	645,954
Servants and Waiters	1,560,721	Merchants and Dealers (except wholesale)	756,802	Laundresses	335,282
Bookkeepers, Clerks, Stenographers, etc.	997,371	Bookkeepers, Clerks, Stenographers, etc.	751,854	Teachers, Professors in Colleges, etc.	327,614
Dressmakers, Milliners, Seamstresses, Tailors, etc.	815,334	Carpenters and Joiners	599,707	Farmers, Planters, and Overseers	307,706
Merchants and Dealers (except wholesale)	790,886	Steam Railroad Employees	580,462	Bookkeepers, Clerks, Stenographers, etc.	245,517
Salesmen and Saleswomen	611,139	Miners and Quarrymen	562,417	Saleswomen	149,230
Carpenters and Joiners	600,252	Draymen, Hackmen, Teamsters	538,029	Laborers (not specified)	123,975
Steam Railroad Employees	582,150	Salesmen	461,909	Cotton Mill Operatives	120,603
Miners and Quarrymen	563,406	Iron and Steel Workers	287,241	Nurses and Midwives	108,691
Draymen, Hackmen, Teamsters, etc.	538,933	Machinists	282,574	Boarding and Lodging House Keepers	59,455
Teachers, Professors in Colleges, etc.	446,133	Painters, Glaziers, and Varnishers	275,782	Musicians and Teachers of Music	52,359

DEMAND FOR WORKERS

Launderers and Laundresses	385,965	Manufacturers and Officials	239,649	Tobacco and Cigar Factory Operatives	43,497
Iron and Steel Workers	290,538	Agents	230,606	Boot and Shoe Makers and Repairers	39,510
Machinists	283,145	Blacksmiths	226,284	Merchants and Dealers (except wholesale)	34,084
Painters, Glaziers, and Varnishers	277,541	Engineers and Firemen (not Locomotive)	223,318	Silk Mill Operatives	32,437
Cotton Mill Operatives	246,391	Boot and Shoe Makers and Repairers	169,393	Shirt, Collar and Cuff Makers	30,941
Manufacturers and Officials	243,009	Dressmakers, Milliners, Tailors, etc.	169,380	Woolen Mill Operatives	30,630
Blacksmiths	226,477	Saw and Planing Mill Employees	161,251	Telegraph and Telephone Operatives	22,556

[1] This table is based on Table IV of the volume on Occupations, U. S. Census, 1900.

TABLE III[1]

Occupations showing the Greatest Growth, for Both Sexes and for Women separately, 1870-1900

BOTH SEXES	1870	1900	INCREASE	WOMEN	1870	1900	INCREASE
Stenographers and Typewriters	154	112,364	729.6 times	Electricians	—	409	
Salesmen and Saleswomen	14,203	611,139	43.0 "	Lawyers	5	1,010	202 times
Officials of Mining and Quarrying Cos.	576[2]	17,355	30.1 "	Bottlers and Soda Water Makers	5	794	158.8 "
Bottlers and Soda Water Makers	458	10,519	22.9 "	Woodchoppers	—	113	
Janitors and Sextons	2,920	56,577	19.3 "	Agents	97	10,556	108.8 "
Silk Mill Operatives	3,256	54,460	16.7 "	Tinplate and Tinware Makers	17	1,775	104.4 "
Clock and Watch Makers and Repairers	1,779	24,120	13.5 "	Packers and Shippers	195	19,988	102.5 "
Street Railway Employees	5,103	68,919	13.5 "	Lumbermen and Raftsmen	—	100	
Hosiery and Knitting Mill Operatives	3,653	47,120	12.9 "	Engineers (civil) and Surgeons	—	84	
Agents	20,316	241,162	11.9 "	Messengers and Errand and Office Girls	80	6,663	83.2 "
Packers and Shippers	5,461	59,545	10.9 "	Architects, Designers, Draftsmen, etc.	14	1,041	74.3 "
Literary and Scientific Persons	1,751	18,844	10.7 "	Clock and Watch Makers and Repairers	75	4,815	64.2 "

Actors, Professional Showmen, etc.	3,230	34,760	10.7 "
Turpentine Farmers and Laborers	2,478	24,735	9.9 "
Nurses and Midwives	12,162	120,956	9.9 "
Telegraph and Telephone Operators	8,316	74,982	9.0 "
Architects, Designers, Draftsmen, etc.	3,303	29,524	8.9 "
Plumbers, Gas and Steam Fitters	11,143	97,785	8.7 "

Telegraph and Telephone Operators	355	22,556	63.5 "
Journalists	35	2,193	62.6 "
Saleswomen [3]	2,775	149,230	53.7 "
Janitors and Sextons	153	8,033	52.5 "
Clergymen	67	3,373	60.3 "
Street Railroad Employees	1	46	46.0 "
Hostlers	2	79	39.5 "
Brewers and Malsters	8	275	34.3 "
Dentists	24	807	33.5 "
Bookkeepers, Clerks, Stenographers	8,023	245,517	30.6 "

[1] Based on Tables III and IV, U. S. Census, 1900, volume on Occupations.

[2] Officials of mining companies only.

[3] Salesmen and saleswomen probably largely returned as clerks in 1870 and 1890 (U. S. Census. Occupations, p. 71)

82 CHOOSING A VOCATION

Sources for the Movement of Demand

For fuller information on Table I refer as follows: —

U. S. Census, 1900. Volume on Occupations, Table XXII. Number of Persons Engaged in Gainful Occupations and in Each Main Class by States and Territories, 1880, 1890, and 1900. Also volumes on Population, Part I, Table VII. Population of States and Territories Arranged Geographically, 1870-1900.

For Tables II and III in this chapter, refer to the Census Tables III and IV in the volume on Occupations. Figures for 1850 are found in Table V in the same volume.

For summaries of the most marked changes shown in the per cent of men and women employed in the different occupations, see volume on Occupations, pp. cxxxvii to cxxxix. See also Table XLVIII. Per cent Distribution of Men, Women, and Children of Persons Engaged in Specified Occupations, 1880, 1900.

Further references which may prove of interest are the following from the volume on Occupations: —

Table XXXIV. Distribution by Specified Occupations of Males and of Females in each Principal Element of the Population Gainfully Employed, 1890-1900.

Table XLIV. Distribution by Sex of Persons Engaged in Specified Occupations in 1900 with per cent Distribution for 1880 and 1890.

Table LXXXVIII. Number of Males in Specified Occupations Unemployed during any Portion of the Census Year, compared with the Total Number of Males so Occupied, 1890 and 1900.

Table LXXXIX. Number of Females in Specified Occupations Unemployed during any Portion of the Census Year, compared with the Total Number of Females so Occupied, 1890 and 1900.

XI

THE GEOGRAPHICAL DISTRIBUTION OF WORKERS IN THE DIFFERENT INDUSTRIES AMONG THE STATES, TERRITORIES, AND CHIEF CITIES OF THE UNITED STATES, 1900

IN finding the geographical distribution throughout the United States of workers in the different industries, two sets of figures will be found useful. First, figures showing the actual numbers employed in the different occupations in the various sections of the country. These will be useful chiefly in such industries as manufacturing, where the demand for workers in a particular section is not necessarily in proportion to the population, and where the chances of the prospective worker are perhaps greater in a section in which already large numbers are employed. In such occupations it will be useful to know the chief geographical centres. This can easily be done by finding, from the figures already mentioned, what state, city, or section of the country employs most workers in the given industry. For instance, we find, in the United States Census for 1900[1] that the chief centre of the glass industry in 1900 was Pennsylvania, where there were 15,765 workmen employed. Indiana, with 10,590 glass workers, came next. Again, in the same way, we find Pennsylvania to be the chief centre of stove, furnace, and grate manufacturing.

Another set of figures would be more directly useful in the case of occupations where the demand for workers is more or less in proportion to population, e. g. in the case of doctors, lawyers, servants, house-painters, etc. In the

[1] Volume on Occupations, Table XXXII.

84 CHOOSING A VOCATION

case of those seeking employment in such occupations, it is obviously well to know what sections are overstocked, and in what places their services are likely to be most in demand. This is one object of the second set of figures, which gives us the number of persons employed in the different occupations per thousand of population in the states, territories, and chief cities of the United States. Unfortunately, as the Census is published only once in every ten years, and these figures therefore cannot be kept up to date, much of their value is lost. They are still of use, however, in showing to what extent a city or state has specialized in any industry, that is, in showing what proportion of the city or state population is employed in the industry given.

The table on pages 86, 87 has been prepared to summarize briefly the geographical distribution of demand, and to illustrate further the purpose of the two sets of figures mentioned. It will be noticed that the South Central and the South Atlantic Division of states employ more persons in agriculture in proportion to their population than any other sections specified (the South Central Division employing 234.4 per thousand, and the South Atlantic 194.6 per thousand). The North Central Division employs only 133.2 per thousand of its population, yet contains actually a greater number of persons in agricultural pursuits than either the South Central or the South Atlantic Divisions.

Thus from the two sets of figures we obtain two kinds of facts. From the figures giving the actual numbers employed, we find to what extent an industry is "localized"; that is, to what sections of the country, to what states, territories, or cities it may be more or less confined, and what per cent of the total number is employed in these geographical centres. Again, we discover from the second set of figures to what extent a given section of the country, a state, territory, or city, may have specialized in certain

DISTRIBUTION OF WORKERS 85

industries, that is, what proportion of the state or city population gainfully employed is engaged in the industries given.

The figures in Table IV are intended to illustrate these points. Of course, in geographical distribution, just as much as in the movement of demand, figures relating to specific industries are of more practical value.

The following are a few striking instances of localization in specified industries. In 1900 turpentine farming was confined wholly to these Southern states, — Alabama, Florida, Georgia, Louisiana, Mississippi, North and South Carolina, which employed all the turpentine farmers and laborers in the country. Georgia, Florida, and Alabama together employed 85.1 per cent of the total number. Georgia alone employed 43.9 per cent.

The silk manufacturing industry was localized chiefly in New Jersey and Pennsylvania. In 1900, 71.1 per cent of the total number of silk mill operatives in the United States were there employed, while 38.3 per cent of the total number were in New Jersey alone.

The states employing the greatest number of quarrymen were Pennsylvania, New York, Ohio, Vermont, Indiana, and Massachusetts; 56.1 per cent of the total number of quarrymen in the country were employed in these states, and 22.4 per cent of the total number in Pennsylvania alone.

The manufacture of boots and shoes, we find, centred chiefly in the following North Atlantic states, — Massachusetts, New Hampshire, New York, and Maine, which together employed 71.4 per cent of the total number of boot and shoe makers and repairers in the United States. Massachusetts alone employed 50.3 per cent.

An instance of specialization in industry is found in Brockton, Mass., where almost one half of the total number of persons gainfully employed come under the heading of "Boot and shoe makers and repairers." Again in Lawrence, Mass., more than one quarter of the total

TABLE IV

The Geografical Distribution of Workers in the Main Classes of Gainful Oppucations

	POPULA-TION[1]	ALL OCCUPATIONS		AGRICULTURE		PROFESSIONAL SERVICE	
		TOTAL NO. EMPLOYED	NO. PER 1000	TOTAL NO. EMPLOYED	NO. PER 1000	TOTAL NO. EMPLOYED	NO. PER 1000
United States[2]	76,303,387	29,073,233	381.08	10,381,765	136.06	1,258,538	16.49
North Atlantic Division	21,046,695	8,579,191	407.62	1,074,412	51.05	411,279	19.54
South Atlantic Division	10,443,480	4,000,531	383.06	2,032,569	194.63	119,360	11.43
North Central Division	26,333,004	9,580,649	363.86	3,508,808	133.25	478,036	18.16
South Central Division	14,080,047	5,209,755	370.00	3,300,817	234.43	152,381	10.82
Western Division	4,091,349	1,703,107	416.27	465,159	113.69	97,482	23.83

DISTRIBUTION OF WORKERS

	DOMESTIC AND PERSONAL SERVICE		TRADE AND TRANSPORTATION		MANUFACTURING AND MECHANICAL	
	TOTAL NO. EMPLOYED	NO. PER 1000	TOTAL NO. EMPLOYED	NO. PER 1000	TOTAL NO. EMPLOYED	NO. PER 1000
United States	5,580,657	73.13	4,766,964	62.47	7,085,309	993.21
North Atlantic Division	1,857,069	88.23	1,867,805	88.75	3,368,626	160.05
South Atlantic Division	798,837	76.49	422,272	40.43	627,493	60.08
North Central Division	1,759,936	66.84	1,671,015	63.46	2,162,854	82.14
South Central Division	793,549	56.36	475,931	33.80	487,077	34.60
Western Division	371,266	90.74	329,941	80.64	439,259	107.36

[1] Total Population for Continental United States.   [2] Continental United States.

88 CHOOSING A VOCATION

number of persons gainfully employed are woolen mill operatives.

Sources

For specific information on these subjects, consult the United States Census for 1900, the volume on Occupations and the volumes on Population, Part I.

For Table IV in this chapter, the following Census Tables were used: —

Volume on Occupations, Table XXII. The Number of Persons Engaged in Gainful Occupations and in Each Main Class by States and Territories, 1880, 1890, and 1900.

Volume on Population, Part I, Table VII. Population of States and Territories Arranged Geographically, 1790-1900.

For all facts regarding specific industries, consult the volume on Occupations, Table XXXII. States and Territories — Total Persons ten years of age and over, engaged in each of 303 specified occupations, 1900.

Table XLII, Principal Cities. Total Males and Females, ten years of age and over employed in each of 140 groups of occupations, for cities having 25,000 inhabitants or more, 1900.

Further references which may prove of interest are as follows: —

Volume on Occupations, Table XLI. Total Males and Females, ten years of age and over Engaged in Selected Groups of Occupations, classified by General Nativity, Color, Conjugal Condition, Months Unemployed, Age periods, and Parentage, by States and Territories, 1900.

Table XLIII the same for cities having 50,000 inhabitants or more. Volumes on Manufacturers, Part I, pp. cxc, ccx, Localization of Industries (determined by value of products).

Table IV, pp. 66-464. Specified Industries by States and Territories, giving facts for each Industry, regarding Number of Establishments, Capital, Power, Number of Proprietors and Firm Members, Number and Salaries of Officials and Clerks; Greatest Number of Wage Earners Employed at any one time during the year; Least Number Employed at any one time during the year.

PART III

THE ORGANIZATION AND THE WORK

XII

THE VOCATION BUREAU

THE Vocation Bureau of Boston was founded in January, 1908, by Mrs. Quincy A. Shaw, on plans drawn up by the writer. More than a dozen years ago I stated the essence of the matter in a lecture on "The Ideal City." That lecture was repeated in Boston before the Economic Club a few years ago, and soon after Mr. Meyer Bloomfield and Mr. Philip Davis, on behalf of the Civic Service House, invited me to speak to the graduating class of one of the evening high schools on the choice of a vocation. After the talk a number of the young men asked for personal interviews, and the results proved to be so helpful that Mr. Bloomfield requested me to draw plans for the permanent organization of the work. These plans were submitted to Mrs. Shaw, who heartily approved the idea, and immediately established the new institution with sufficient resources to enable the work to be begun as a new department of the Civic Service House in the North End of Boston.

Although the work is very young and a good deal of time in these few months has been consumed in the process of organization, a large number of men and women from fifteen to seventy-two years of age have come to us for consultation, and, according to their own statements, all but two have received much light and help, some even declaring that the interview with the counselor was the most important hour of their lives. Among the applicants have been Harvard seniors, students from Dartmouth and other neighboring colleges, a

90 CHOOSING A VOCATION

number of college graduates, young men in commercial and business life, and some older ones, including an ex-bank-president of splendid ability, and a traveling salesman who at one time made sales amounting to two hundred thousand dollars a year.

The majority of applicants, however, have been boys and girls from the high schools or working boys and girls of high school age.

A Vocation Department has been established by the Boston Young Men's Christian Association as a branch of the Bureau, and the counselor has kept regular appointments at the Women's Educational and Industrial Union and at the Twentieth Century Club.

The Bureau does not attempt to decide for any boy what occupation he should choose, but aims to help him investigate the subject and come to a conclusion on his own account, that is much more likely to be valid and useful than if no effort were made to apply scientific methods to the problem. Our mottoes are Light, Information, Inspiration, Coöperation.

XIII

THE SCHOOL FOR VOCATIONAL COUNSELORS

THE Vocation Department of the Boston Young Men's Christian Association has established a school for vocational counselors, to train men for carrying on vocational bureau work in connection with Young Men's Christian Associations, schools, colleges, universities, social settlements, and business establishments. The employment department of the Y. M. C. A. acts in coördination with the vocation department.

The demand for vocational counselors able to do the kind of work described in the preceding sections is growing very rapidly. The present staff of workers is wholly inadequate to the need of this city alone, and the widespread practical interest in the new institution justifies the belief that the movement will soon become a national one. The prospects are that vocational guidance will be made a part of the service of the Y. M. C. A.'s and other educational institutions in all our principal cities, as fast as competent men can be secured.

To fit men for this new vocation, this pioneer school for the training of counselors has been established.

The work consists of lectures, research, practice by the laboratory method, reports of results, conferences, discussions and special tests subject to the criticism of the instructor and the members of the class. At least three hours a week are given by each member to this laboratory practice, examining applicants for vocational advice, and formulating the counsel believed to be appropriate for the solution of the specific problem presented by each case.

CHOOSING A VOCATION

Members are called upon from time to time to examine applicants in the presence of the class, and then (after the applicant has retired) they analyze the facts obtained, and state the points of counsel and suggestion they think the case calls for. The presence of the instructor and the class, and their observations, questions, and criticisms, upon the proceedings, give this sort of practice the highest educational value. Practical talks by leading business and professional men and representatives of important industrial interests will also constitute an important feature of the course.

To enter the vocational course a man must have excellent character and ability, good manners and address, at least a high school education or its equivalent, and a satisfactory experience of two years or more in teaching or business or social work, or a satisfactory equivalent for such experience. And he must have attained the age of twenty-five years, unless very mature at an earlier age.

The time required will be one, two, or three terms, according to the ability and previous preparation of the student. A certificate of proficiency will be given at the end of any term in which the practical results achieved by the particular student justify his enrollment as an expert, qualified to test the abilities and capacities of young men, apply good judgment, common sense, and scientific method to the various problems a vocation bureau has to deal with, and give appropriate counsel with the insight, sympathy, grasp, and suggestiveness the service calls for.

In addition to mature judgment, a character and personality that invite respect and confidence, and a good general education, including some knowledge of history, civics, and economics, a vocational counselor should possess: (1) A practical working knowledge of the fundamental principles and methods of modern psychology. (2) An experience involving sufficient human contact to give him an intimate acquaintance with human nature in a considerable number

SCHOOL FOR VOCATIONAL COUNSELORS   93

of its different types and phases; he must understand the dominant motives, interests, and ambitions that control the lives of men, and be able to recognize the symptoms that indicate the presence or absence of important elements of character. (3) Ability to deal with young people in a sympathetic, earnest, searching, candid, helpful, and attractive way. Sympathy, candor, and a genuine desire to be of service are the primary elements here; but tact, intellectual grasp, and a sort of inventiveness, or suggestiveness that is near of kin to it, are also essential factors. (4) A knowledge of requirements and conditions of success, compensation, prospects, advantages, and disadvantages, etc., in the different lines of industry. (5) Information relating to courses of study and means of preparing for various callings and developing efficiency therein. (6) Scientific method — analysis and the principles of investigation by which laws and causes are ascertained, facts are classified, and correct conclusions drawn. The counselor must be able to recognize the essential facts and principles involved in each case, group them according to their true relations, and draw the conclusions they justify.

XIV

SUPPLEMENTARY HELPS

Most of the material which has hitherto been used by the Bureau has already been given and described in these chapters. Much additional help will occur to any inventive or inquiring person who undertakes this work.

It is important to have abundant material relating to *apprenticeship methods* of training. The counselor also should have full information about the *vocation schools* of his own and other states. He should tabulate all the day and evening courses given in his community that have a vocational bearing, noting the opportunities for self-support while studying, so that young men and women can see at a glance all the educational advantages that bear upon their problems. Local and class *employment agencies* should be thoroughly studied, and the "help wants" of newspapers should be practiced upon until the counselor is thoroughly familiar with their general nature.

If the counselor finds the *memory* of the applicant below the standard, he gives the youth a printed analysis of the means of developing the memory and securing the best results from it, with a little talk to emphasize the importance of memory and method as the foundations of mastery, grasp, and efficient performance.

A leaflet called "Suggestions for a Plan of Life" is also given in many cases, with oral instructions sufficient to make it vital to the recipient. It is intended to direct attention to the elements essential to an all-round, symmetrical develop-

SUPPLEMENTARY HELPS 95

ment, and the value of making a good plan and living up to it instead of drifting through life like a rudderless boat.

Not less important is the work done in the direction of developing *civic interest*. The boy is impressed with the fact that he is, or soon will be, one of the directors and rulers of the United States, that his part in civic affairs is quite as important as his occupation, vital as that undoubtedly is, that all-round manhood should be the aim, that making a living is only one arc of the circle, and that he must study to be a good citizen as well as a good worker.

The Bureau's leaflets entitled "Civic Suggestions," "Lincoln's Message to Young Men," and "Analysis of Parliamentary Law," are very useful in this connection. The latter enables the young man to fit himself with very little effort to join in the discussions of a town meeting, young men's congress, or debating society, or preside over a meeting with credit to himself if called to the chair. Very often the youth can be led to read and analyze a series of good books on government and public questions, beginning perhaps with Dole and Fiske on Citizenship and Civil Government, or with Bryce's "American Commonwealth," and continuing with the works of Albert Shaw, Zueblin, Howe, and Steffens, the famous speeches of Wendell Phillips, and the messages of Lincoln, Washington, and Roosevelt, the important problem books, such as "The Truth About the Trusts," "Wealth against Commonwealth," "Labor Copartnership," "The Story of New Zealand," etc., and some of the principal books on history, economics, and sociology.

To those who are just starting a vocation bureau the four leaflets, "To Young People," "To Workers," "To Employers," and "Instruction to Those Desiring the Service of the Bureau," will be helpfully suggestive.

Copies of some of these supplementary helps are printed herewith: —

CHOOSING A VOCATION

TO EMPLOYERS

The percentage of inefficiency and change you may experience in your working force, and the cost it entails in employment expense, waste of training, and low-grade service, are largely due to the haphazard way by which young men and women drift into this or that employment, with little or no regard to adaptability, and without adequate preparation or any definite aim or well-considered plan to insure efficiency, devotion, and development.

This Bureau constitutes the first attempt to take practical steps to remedy these conditions through expert counsel and guidance in the selection of a vocation, the preparation for it and the transition from school to work.

In its efforts to aid workers develop their efficiency and improve their condition, and assist those about to select a vocation to choose wisely, prepare carefully, and find opportunities of employment in lines of industry to which they are adapted, this Bureau invites your coöperation.

The principal methods employed in our work are: —

1. *Self-Analysis.* The applicant is made to realize clearly his aptitudes, abilities, ambitions, preparation, resources, and limitations, and to see their relation to the requirements and conditions of success in various callings. As it is, few ever sit down with pencil and paper, with expert information and counsel, to plan a working career and deal with the life problem scientifically, as they would deal with the problem of building a house, taking the advice of an architect to help them.

2. *Information* in respect to the conditions of success in different industries, the initial requirements, compensation, immediate and prospective, and the means of preparation and development, is an important part of our work; as is also specific information as to opportunities in various lines of work, so that young people may be aided in placing themselves rightly, and employers may be aided in securing the type of ability and character they need for specific work. The social and industrial benefits of a more careful correlation of opportunity and ability are incalculable. We are just drifting to-day with planless methods of adapting and distributing labor, both skilled and unskilled.

3. *Stimulation* is equally important. There are fine ambitions in every youth, which if sought out and fed with knowledge and

SUPPLEMENTARY HELPS   97

sympathy will grow strong and clear enough to control the life. Show a man *how* to improve his efficiency and social and economic value, and the benefits that will result, and give him appreciation in his efforts, and he generally needs no urging to adopt the means of self-development.

4. *Coöperation.* The Bureau will actively coöperate with the applicant in his efforts to secure the training he may need, and to find employment for which he is fitted or shall fit himself.

5. *Systematic Guidance and Help,* which ordinarily do not extend beyond the school life, are continued by the Vocation Bureau into the working life, so that there may be no break or gulf between the school and work, but a smooth, clear path from one to the other, with a definite plan for the future, more adeuate preparation for the work to be done, and more efficient performance of it. We care for the children with great solicitude till they are out of the grammar or high school and then drop them into this complex world, with practically no industrial information or foresight, to sink or swim, as the case may be. There is really no time of life when more careful counsel and instruction are needed than in the transition from school to work.

In short, the aim of the Bureau is intelligent, well-directed, scientific choice of occupation and adaptation to it, so far as circumstances permit, instead of haphazard, planless choice, by chance or whim, or uninformed selection, and needlessly imperfect adaptation in many cases, resulting in a great number of misfits and a large degree of inefficiency.

The Bureau specially asks the coöperation of employers in securing as full and definite information as possible regarding the opportunities offered by different industries and the conditions of success therein, and in affording opportunities for the Secretary or other representatives of the Bureau to speak to groups of employees and make appointments with them for individual conference and consultation.

TO WORKERS

If you wish expert counsel in the analysis of your possibilities and the conditions of success in your line of effort, and in the selection and adoption of the best means for achieving the fullest success of which you are capable, this Bureau will gladly aid you

CHOOSING A VOCATION

for the good that will come to you and to the public from the development of your economic value and the improvement of your industrial condition. Its services are free. It is part of the social work of the Civic Service House in coöperation with the Young Men's Christian Association, the Economic Club, and the Women's Educational and Industrial Union.

If you find that you are not adapted to the work in which you are engaged, the Bureau will aid you in determining what occupation may be better suited to your capacities and powers, and in selecting the best available means of preparing for it and building up a successful career.

TO YOUNG PEOPLE

STUDENTS AND OTHERS CONSIDERING THE QUESTION OF THEIR LIFE WORK

The wise selection of the business, profession, trade, or occupation, to which you are to devote yourself, and the building of a successful career in your chosen vocation, are matters of great moment to you and to the public. These vital problems should be solved in a careful, scientific way, with due regard to your aptitudes, abilities, ambitions, resources, and limitations, and the relations of these elements to the conditions of success in different industries. Definite knowledge of yourself and of the opportunities, requirements, compensation, immediate and prospective, etc., in various callings, is essential. Systematic information as to the best means of preparation within your reach, and the methods by which others have succeeded, is also most desirable.

This Bureau was established to help you in all these matters by counsel, guidance, information, and coöperation. Its services are free.

Many have already been greatly helped in the ways suggested — helped to find their true vocation, — the business or occupation to which their abilities and resources best adapt them, and to find an opening in that vocation and the means of attaining efficiency and success; and the experience of each of these young men and women helps to light the way for others.

The guidance given in school days generally ceases when the

SUPPLEMENTARY HELPS   99

student leaves the grammar school or high school or college to begin work. Yet there is really no time of life when wise counsel and expert assistance are more needful than in the transition from school to the new life of labor.

No one would think of building a dwelling or a business block without carefully selecting an appropriate and advantageous site and drawing a well-considered plan with the help of an architect or expert builder. And in building a career it is quite as important to make a wise location, lay the foundations properly, and work up by a well-considered, scientific plan.

It is better to sail with compass and chart than to drift into an occupation haphazard or by chance, proximity, or uninformed selection; and drift on through it without reaching any port worthy of the voyage.

SUGGESTIONS FOR A PLAN OF LIFE[1]

Study the LAWS and CAUSES of things and of human action, grasp PRINCIPLES as well as FACTS, and attend most carefully to METHOD, SYSTEM, PROPORTION, and DEVELOPMENT in relation to the various life values noted in the following analysis.

Health: *Fresh air*, life is combustion; the furnace blast, deep breathing, open windows. *Good food*, well chewed; in due quantity and variety. *Exercise*, moral duty to perspire each day. *Bathing. Rest. Clothing* warm and easy. *Good society; good nature; clear conscience; earnest purpose.*

Activity: Amount and quality Proportion of different varieties; differences between nations and individuals.

Development of power, ability, and character, by systematic, persistent effort under the laws of habit and reflex action.

Mind: Memory, reason, imagination. Observe, read, converse, analyze, and digest. Search for laws and causes. Learn the methods of discovering truth, and arriving at correct conclusions. Test your results again and again. Absorb the best books. Study psychology and the laws of human nature so as to understand yourself and others. Organize your knowledge. Marshal your facts and principles in companies and battalions under your command. Reduce what you learn to its lowest terms, master it and use it. Cultivate imaginative power and inventiveness. Watch the inner light. Keep curiosity alive, and avail yourself of scientific method.

Character: Truth, sympathy, justice. Be honest, truthful, reliable, prompt, effective. Keep your engagements. Be just, receptive, open-minded, and tolerant, but do your own thinking. Be reasonably consistent. Be candid, kindly, sympathetic, coöperative, progressive, good natured, cheerful, industrious, methodical, persistent, hopeful, modest.

Longevity

Power

Growth
of body,
mind,
and soul.

Education
life-long,
for power,
not for exams.

Enthusiasm
tempered
with
moderation
and
self-control.

Simplicity,
Certainty,
Breadth.

Symmetry,
proportion,
adaptation,
emphasis.

Coördination
and balance.
Regard
substance and
cause
more than
form and
circumstance.

Keep sweet
and
do right.
Morals
summed up
in the
Golden Rule.

DON'T
be too
familiar
with ice water,
tea, coffee,
tobacco, or
alcoholics.
Avoid excess,
dissipation, and
disease; and
be very careful
about drugs
and doctors.

DON'T be
idle, sluggish,
inattentive,
non-progressive.

AVOID
ill-logic,
prejudice
bigotry,
empty-mindedness,
hasty conclusions,
wrong methods
of observation
and reasoning.

DON'T read
trash.

DON'T be stubborn,
surly,
pugilistic,
unruly,
careless,
unreceptive,
unreliable,
dishonest.

[1] *Copyright*, 1905, *by Frank Parsons.*

SUPPLEMENTARY HELPS 101

C.Z. Avoid in yourself what you do not like in others. Develop desirable elements of character by daily practice, just as you develop your muscles and your mental faculties. And get your friends to help you by calling your attention to defects in your character.

Occupation. Choose your occupation carefully and master it thoroughly. Make money, but don't worship it or be a slave to it. Money is for life, not life for money.

Recreation: Make it a balance to your work.

Manners. Repeat C. Z. here, changing *"character"* to *"manners."*

Accomplishments. Conversation as a fine art. The tunes of speech. The beauty that shines through from within.

Relationships: Friendship, marriage, family life, citizenship, business and social life.
Exercise good judgment, care, common sense, and system, as well as emotion, in them all. Care is quite as necessary in choosing a wife or a husband as in choosing a horse. And bringing up a child is quite as complex and difficult, and needs quite as much preparation, as running a locomotive. Citizenship also demands your best thought; understand the movements of your age and the questions of your day, and do your duty as a civic partner.

Ideals: Individual and social, quiescent and active, subordinate and dominant.
Ideals have power to mould your life and the laws and institutions of your country. Every great movement in history was an ideal before it became a fact. Be careful to form true ideals, and help others to do likewise, — ideals in harmony with justice and humanity, — and *apply* your ideals as far as you can in business, politics, and social life as well as in your home.

Happiness,
— the pleasures of sense,
— "the joy of doing,"
— the pleasures of possession,
— the pleasures of the intellect,
— the joys of sympathy and love,
— the delights of devotion to high purpose.

Not self-sacrifice, but sacrifice of the lower self to the higher self is the secret.

Power
Service
Love
Beauty
Humor
Lofty aim.

History
Biography
Fiction
Poetry
Oratory
Music and Art

Work
Play
Children
Animals
Men and Women

Nature
Science
Home, Business
School, Gov't
Church, Society
Theatre, Travel.

Service
in sympathy, love, and devotion.

Not aggressive individualism but ennobled coöperative individualism.

Brotherhood and Mutualism, not conquest and mastery.

DON'T be
unjust,
unkind,
thoughtless,
stupid,
pessimistic,
grumbly,
cruel,
unsympathetic,
overbearing,
discourteous,
hasty,
intolerant,
unreasonable,
untrue,
silly,
conceited,
intemperate,
double-faced,
avaricious,
snobbish,
bombastic,
dudish,
dissipated,
over-critical,
unmannerly,
mean,
despondent,
dogmatic,
despotic,
rash,
ungenerous,
selfish,
slow,
disorderly,
deceitful,
destructive,
disobedient,
tardy,
inefficient,
cowardly,
vacillating,
over-confident,
over-aggressive,
hypocritical,
self-deceived.

102 CHOOSING A VOCATION

MEMORY[1]

LAWS AND METHODS OF ITS USE AND CULTIVATION

Physical Basis. Physiological retentiveness, gray matter of reasonable consistency.
Quality improved by attention to conditions of health and strength and by specific exercise.

Selection. Can't remember everything.

Analysis.
Substance; vital facts and principles.
Condensation; reduce substance to lowest terms, and label with key words.
Form; arrange according to relations of sequence, cause, subordination, etc.; make an analytic digest, diagram, or picture.

Association. The physiological law of memory.
1. Tie the new thought with some other idea or ideas already firmly fixed in the mind, or of deep interest to you.
2. Classify, link with like facts, or with contrasts; tie your facts in bundles.

Registration. 1. In best centre.
2. Multiple registration in visual, auditory, speaking, and writing centres.
3. Time and method.

Attention. Focus the mind on the things to be memorized; concentrate.

Emphasis. Physical tension to deepen impression.

Repetition. To wear a deeper channel and form a habit in the gray cells.

Reflection. Let the mind DWELL on the matter, roll it over and over, look at it on all sides, draw inferences from it, etc.

Use, Expression, Exercise at high temperature or in emotional atmosphere.
Tell what you wish to remember to some one in whom you feel a strong interest, or under circumstances stirring your emotions. Use it in your business or play, Build on it a course of study or conduct, or some undertaking.
Have companionship in your studies and memorizing, etc.

SPECIAL HINTS

1. Don't wash out ideas and diminish retentiveness with a flood of transient impressions.
2. Don't exhaust the bloom; German language method.
3. Don't cram.
4. Take advantage of the law of unconscious cerebration,
Bed time, meal time, etc,
5. Take advantage of the psychologic laws of interest, habit, reflex action — the increase of power and pleasure with practice.
At a given time each day if possible run over valuable analyses in thought till they FLASH through your mind in volumes.
6. Form or join magazine club or culture club to divide labor of selection and analysis and secure the stimulus and emotional emphasis of companionship.
7. Use key words constantly in sets.
8. Use memoranda — make paper memory save the mind on non-essentials, and back up the brain record with unchangeable written records of essentials.

[1] *Copyright,* 1904, *by Frank Parsons.*

SUPPLEMENTARY HELPS 103

CIVIC SUGGESTIONS

No matter how successful a man may be in business, no matter how much money he may make, nor how honest and efficient he may be industrially, if he is not a good citizen, fully alive to all his civic rights, privileges, duties, and responsibilities, he is no more than half a man at best. A man who exerts himself only to get his bread and butter, and not at all for the social good, has not developed much beyond the oyster stage of civilization, although in outward appearance he may resemble a real human being.

Your part in civic life is quite as important as your occupation, vital as that undoubtedly is. All round manhood is the true aim. Making a living is only one arc of the circle. You must be a good citizen as well as a good worker. You do not want to be alive only on one side and dead on the other. You are one of the directors and rulers of these United States, or soon will be, and you should know how public business is transacted, understand the great questions that are before the people, and do your share in securing good government and civic improvement, and promoting true solutions of the vital problems of the day. A few specific suggestions on these lines may be of use to you.

1. Visit the Legislature now and then, and the City Council or Town Meeting, to observe the process of manufacturing laws and ordinances. Attend the hearings on important measures before legislative committees. The legislators are your servants, and you should know how they do their work, and whether they are doing it right or not. Get the Municipal Register at City Hall and the Manual of the General Court at the State House.

2. Go to the Superior Court and see a jury trial in a civil case. Then visit the Supreme Court and hear a case argued before the full bench. The sessions of the Federal Courts in the Post Office Building should also be visited. After you have seen the process of enforcing the law by judicial procedure, you may be interested to go to the Law Library at the State House and read some decisions rendered in famous cases by the Massachusetts Supreme Court or the Supreme Court of the United States.

3. Attend important lectures and discussions of political and economic problems, and if possible join some organization where public questions are discussed, — the Economic Club, City Club,

104 CHOOSING A VOCATION

Twentieth Century Club, Civic Service House Forum, Y. M. C. A. Congress, or any good debating club, — and take part in the discussions.

4. Read the summaries of current events and political opinion in some of the best magazines, such as *The Review of Reviews, The Arena, The Outlook, The Literary Digest, The Public, The World's Work,* etc. Study the collections of cartoons in the first two. And read the civic editorials in at least one good newspaper representing each of the great divisions of political thought and organization.

5. Send letters to the press expressing your views on public affairs. Write also to the Mayor and Governor and other city or state officials, and to your representatives in City Hall, at the State House and in Washington, so that they may know you are watching them and may have at hand a record of your views for or against important measures, and the reasons for your attitude. The greater the number of citizens who will do such civic work as this in patriotic and enlightened performance of their duties as national, state, and municipal directors, the more complete will be the record of public sentiment available for the guidance of legislators and officials, and the greater their incentive to honest and energetic action for the public good in the light of the watchful interest of an enlightened citizenship.

6. Notify the Board of Health of any stagnant water, rubbish heaps, unsanitary buildings, contagious diseases, impure foods, or other unhealthful conditions you observe. True patriotism begins at home, with care for our own neighborhood.

7. To form a solid basis for your own independent thinking and usefulness as a citizen, study some of the best books on citizen ship, government, economics, and the principal public questions of the day. Take also, if you can, a course in political science, economics, and sociology. There are evening classes for those who cannot study in the daytime.

Select some good books from the following list in consultation with the counselor, and begin a systematic course of analytic reading on government, economics, history, and the leading problems that are before the people for discussion and solution.

"The American Citizen": Charles F. Dole.
"The Young Citizen": Charles F. Dole.

SUPPLEMENTARY HELPS 105

"The Spirit of Democracy": Charles F. Dole.
"Civic Reader for New Americans": Meyer Bloomfield,
C. F. Dole, and others.
"Civil Government in the United States": John Fiske.
"Advanced Civics": Forman.
"The Government": S. S. Clark.
"Civil Government": George H. Martin.
"American Political Ideals": John Fiske.
"The American Commonwealth": James Bryce.
"Municipal Government in Great Britain": Albert Shaw.
"Municipal Government in Continental Europe": Albert Shaw.
"The State": Woodrow Wilson.
"Democracy and Social Ethics": Jane Addams.

Lincoln's Gettysburg Address.
Washington's Farewell Address.
The Messages of President Roosevelt.

> A powerful presentation of progressive measures, trust and labor
> legislation, control of corporations, industrial arbitration, income and
> inheritance taxes, postal savings banks, etc.

"World Politics": Paul S. Reinsch.
"World Organization": Raymond Bridgman.
"Organize the World": Edwin D. Mead.
"Patriotism and the New Internationalism": Lucia Ames
Mead.

"General History": Myers.
"Modern History": Myers.
United States History: John Fiske's volumes.
"Short History of the English People": Greene.
"Europe in the Nineteenth Century": Judson.
"The Wonderful Century": Wallace.

> An inspiring account of the great inventions and achievements of
> the nineteenth century.

"Great Movements of the Nineteenth Century": Parsons.
"Story of New Zealand": Parsons.

> How New Zealand established industrial arbitration, old-age pen-
> sions, public coal mines, progressive land-value, income and inheri-
> tance taxes, postal savings banks, government loan offices, public
> ownership of the money system, government railroads, national
> employment bureau, public insurance, etc.

106 CHOOSING A VOCATION

"How England Averted a Revolution": Flower.

> A campaign of education by pamphlet and platform in the corn law agitation, saved a resort to force.

"The Federalist": Senator Lodge's Edition.

Washington, Jefferson, Hamilton, Sumner, and others in American Statesmen Series.
"Speeches and Lectures": Wendell Phillips.
"Short Life of Abraham Lincoln": Nicolay.
"Autobiography of Benjamin Franklin."
"Theodore Roosevelt": Jacob Riis.

"Outlines of Economics": R. T. Ely.
"Principles of Economics": E. R. A. Seligman.
"Political Economy": Francis A. Walker.
"Principles of Economics": Alfred Marshall.
"Institutes of Economics": Andrews.
"The New Political Economy": Parsons.
"Labor Copartnership": Henry D. Lloyd.
"Distribution of Wealth": John R. Commons.
"Economics of Distribution": John A. Hobson.
"Evolution of Modern Capitalism": John A. Hobson.
"The Truth About the Trusts": John Moody.
"The Trust Problem": J. W. Jenks.
"Wealth Against the Commonwealth": Henry D. Lloyd.

> The Story of Standard Oil.

"History of the Standard Oil Trust": Ida M. Tarbell.
"Chapters of Erie": Charles Francis Adams.
"The Railways, the Trusts, and the People": Parsons.
"The Strategy of Great Railroads": Spearman.
"The Railway Question": Stickney.
"The Railroad Question": Larrabee.
"National Consolidation of Railways": Lewis.
"A General Freight and Passenger Post": Cowles.

"Municipal Monopolies": Bemis, Commons, Parsons, and others.
"The City for the People": Parsons.

> Public Ownership, Direct Legislation, Direct Nominations, Proportional Representation, Preferential Voting, Home Rule for Cities, The Ideal City Charter.

SUPPLEMENTARY HELPS 107

Public Ownership Report of National Civic Federation Commission, especially the summaries in volume i.

"The Shame of the Cities": Lincoln Steffens.
"The City the Hope of Democracy": Frederick C. Howe.
"American Municipal Progress": Charles Zueblin.
"How the Other Half Lives" : Jacob Riis.
"The Battle with the Slum": Jacob Riis.
"The Improvement of Towns and Cities": Charles M. Robinson.
"The City Wilderness": Robert A. Woods and others.
"Americans in Process": Robert A. Woods and others.

"Up from Slavery": Booker T. Washington.
"Progress and Poverty": Henry George.
"Looking Backward": Edward Bellamy.
"Merrie England": Robert Blatchford.
"An Inquiry into Socialism": Thomas Kirkup.
"Socialism and Social Reform": Richard T. Ely.
"Bi-Socialism"": Oliver Trowbridge.
"Social Unrest": John Graham Brooks.
"New Worlds for Old": H. G. Wells.
"The Foundations of Sociology": Edward A. Ross.
"Social Control": Edward A. Ross.
"Practical Sociology": Carroll D. Wright.
"Dynamic Sociology": Lester F. Ward.

To find articles in leading magazines for any subject you are studying, refer to "Poole's Index" and "The Reader's Guide" in the periodical room at the Public Library.

For reference purposes you should also acquaint yourself with —

The World Almanac.
The Statesman's Year Book.
The Municipal Year Book (English).
The Australian Handbook.
The Annals of the American Academy of Political and Social Science.
Reports of the National Municipal League, the League of American Municipalities, and the National Civic Federation.
Bliss's "Cyclopedia of Social Reform" (Edition of 1908).

CHOOSING A VOCATION

Mulhall's "Dictionary of Statistics."

Poor's "Railroad Manual."

Interstate Commerce Commission Reports.

Bulletins of the U. S. Department of Commerce and Labor.

The Congressional Record.

Proceedings of the House and Senate and Reports of Committees.

"Who's Who in America."

The Century Dictionary.

The Universal Cyclopedia, and

The American and English Encyclopedia of Law.

XV

SAMPLE CASES

EXPERIENCE is the great teacher. I shall be glad if my experience in this line of work can become valuable to others. I keep a record of each case. If it is not worth putting down on paper, it is not worth doing at all. Not until I have written out a summary of the case can I feel that I have done it anything like adequate justice. The following selected cases illustrate the wide variety of method and treatment: —

Case 3

A CARTOONIST IN THE BUD

A working boy of eighteen, graduate of a Boston high school, said he wanted to be a cartoonist. He was strong, healthy, energetic, and enthusiastic. He had a fine, expressive face, clear, keen eye, and pleasing manners. He stood the memory test excellently well, showed some imagination and inventiveness, and a good deal of skill with his pencil. He had done some good reading on his own account, solid books of history and science.

The counselor saw no reason why he should not be aided and encouraged in the pursuit of his ambition to become a cartoonist. The suggestions of the counselor, therefore, related chiefly to method.

Suggestions.

1. Get large scrapbooks, or make them for yourself out of manilla paper.

110 CHOOSING A VOCATION

2. Get your friends to give you copies of *The Review of Reviews* and other magazines and newspapers that publish the best cartoons. Cut them out. Classify them according to the principles involved, just as naturalists classify animals and plants. Paste them in your scrapbooks, putting those of each class together. Mark each one with a word or phrase which will be to you the name of that cartoon. Make a list of these words and phrases that you can carry in your pocket.

Turn over the leaves of your scrapbook every day, and two or three times a day if you can. Study the best cartoons carefully, and after each study shut your eyes or look at the ceiling and see if you can recall the picture. Sketch the cartoons from memory, taking one at a time, drawing it over and over again, comparing your sketch each time with the original, and correcting your work until you can make a good sketch of each of the best cartoons from memory.

When you are in the cars or anywhere else, with a few moments' leisure, take out your list of words and phrases representing your cartoon specimens and try to flash before your mind rapidly the pictures corresponding to the words and phrases on your list.

In other words, *master* your collection of good cartoons; put them in your brain and at your fingers' ends. They constitute for you the a b c of your profession, and you must make them a part of yourself, master them as thoroughly as you did the multiplication table when you studied arithmetic.

3. Look at the headlines of the leading papers every day, and every two or three days, or once a week at least, select some subject that interests you strongly, and try to represent your thought of it in cartoon form, using pictures of men and animals, etc., to express your meaning, as the cartoonists do.

SAMPLE CASES   111

If your thought does not readily flow into picture form, turn the pages of your cartoon books, looking at each picture with the thought you wish to express clearly in your mind, and see if you do not get a suggestion from some of the cartoons in your books.

Draw your cartoon and compare it with those in your books, especially those of the same class, principle, or method of work. Then see if you can improve your drawing; and when you get it so that you are satisfied with it or believe it to be the best you can make it at that time, take it to some artist friend and get him to criticise it. Correct it in the light of his suggestions if you think they are well founded, and then send it to some newspaper or magazine that prints cartoons and see if they will publish it. If not, send it to another, and another, keeping on until you get it published, or are pretty sure you cannot place it.

Do this every week, or as often as you conveniently can, and after a while, with careful and persistent and well-directed effort, you will be practically sure to succeed.

The counselor will be glad to see your drawings from time to time and make such further suggestions as may seem best, and also help you get acquainted with some artist competent to criticise your work.

4. While you are studying and working on the direct lines of your intended vocation, do not neglect the advantages to be secured by continued reading of the best books, especially those on history, economics, and natural science, with Emerson's "Essays" and some good poetry. Such reading will not only help you to develop into a first-class man all round, a good citizen and respected member of society, — which is quite as important as being a good cartoonist, — but it will also help you in your profession by filling your mind with vivid images of many kinds, and giving you the power to appreciate the significance and

CHOOSING A VOCATION

relationships of public questions and current events. A man cannot be a first-class workman at any trade or profession unless he knows a good deal more than the special matters involved in his business. He must master the technic of his profession, and he must also know a good deal about the world in general, and human nature in particular, in order that he may understand the relations between his special work and the varied interests of his fellow men.

Case 6

A WOULD-BE DOCTOR

A boy of nineteen said he wanted to be a doctor. He was sickly looking, small, thin, hollow-cheeked, with listless eye and expressionless face. He did not smile once during the interview of more than an hour. He shook hands like a wet stick. His voice was husky and unpleasant, and his conversational power, aside from answering direct questions, seemed practically limited to "ss-uh," an aspirate "yes, sir," consisting of a prolonged s followed by a non-vocal uh, made by suddenly dropping the lower jaw and exploding the breath without bringing the vocal cords into action. He used this aspirate "yes-sir" constantly, to indicate assent, or that he heard what the counselor said. He had been through the grammar school and the evening high; was not good in any of his studies, nor especially interested in any. His memory was poor. He fell down on all the tests for mental power. He had read practically nothing outside of school except the newspapers. He had no resources and very few friends. He was not tidy in his appearance, nor in any way attractive. He knew nothing about a doctor's life; not even that he might have to get up any time in the middle of the night, or that he had to remember books full of symptoms and remedies.

SAMPLE CASES 113

The boy had no enthusiasms, interests, or ambitions except the one consuming ambition to be something that people would respect, and he thought he could accomplish that purpose by becoming a physician more easily than in any other way.

When the study was complete, and the young man's record was before him, the counselor said : —

"Now we must be very frank with each other. That is the only way such talks can be of any value. You want me to tell you the truth just as I see it, don't you? That's why you came to me, is n't it, — not for flattery, but for a frank talk to help you understand yourself and your possibilities?"

"Ss-uh."

"Don't you think a doctor should be well and strong? Does n't he need vigorous health to stand irregular hours, night calls, exposure to contagious diseases, etc.?"

"Ss-uh."

"And you are not strong."

"Ss-uh." (This was repeated after almost every sentence of the counselor's remarks, but will be omitted here for the sake of condensation.)

"And you have n't the pleasant manners a doctor ought to have. You have not smiled nor shown any expressiveness in your face the whole time you have been answering my questions and telling me about your life and record. Your hand was moist and unpleasant when you shook hands. And you put your fingers in my hand without any pressure, or show of interest. I might as well have shaken hands with a stick."

(The counselor's criticisms were very frank and forceful, but he smiled at the boy as he spoke, and his tones were quite gentle and sympathetic, so that the young man was not offended or repelled, but seemed attracted and pleased, on the whole, by the frank and kindly interest of the counselor in his welfare.)

114 CHOOSING A VOCATION

"You might cultivate a cordial smile, a friendly handshake, and winning manners, and you ought to develop good manners no matter what business you follow, but it will take much time and effort, for manners do not come natural to you.

"You should cultivate your voice, and use smooth, clear tones, with life in them. Your voice is listless, husky, and unpleasant now.

"And read good solid books, — history, economics, government, etc., — and talk about them. Develop your conversational power. At present you do not even seem able to say, 'yes, sir,' distinctly.

"You want to win respect, to be something your fellow men will admire. But it is not necessary to be a doctor in order to be respectable.

"Any man who lives a useful life, does his work well, takes care of his family, is a good citizen, and lives a clean, true, kindly, helpful life, will be respected and loved, whether he is a farmer, carpenter, lawyer, doctor, blacksmith, teamster, clerk, or factory worker.

"People will respect a carpenter who knows his business and does his work well a good deal more than they will a doctor who does n't know his business. It is a question of fitness, knowledge, skill, and usefulness. A bad doctor is one of the least respectable of men. Think of the blunders he is likely to make, the people he is likely to kill or injure through wrong medicines or lack of skill in diagnosis or treatment."

The counselor then painted two word pictures substantially as follows: —

"Suppose two men are trying to build up a medical practice. One is tall, fine looking, strong, and healthy, with a winning smile, a cordial way of shaking hands, pleasant voice, and engaging manners. He is bright, cheery, wholesome. People like to have him visit them. His

SAMPLE CASES 115

presence in the sickroom is a tonic worth as much as the medicine he gives. He has a good education, has read a lot of good books, keeps posted in the leading magazines, and understands the public questions of the day, so he can talk to all sorts of people about the things that interest them. He has a good memory, so he can carry in his mind the volumes of symptoms and medical data a doctor ought to know, and can tell a case of smallpox, scarlet fever, diphtheria, etc., etc., without running back to his office to study the books. He has friends to help him get patients, and money enough to live in good style three or four years while he is building up a practice.

"The other man is small, thin, hollow cheeked, sickly looking, with poor memory, little education, practically no reading, no resources, undeveloped manners, husky, unpleasant voice, no conversational ability, — nothing to attract people or inspire their confidence, and with mental handicaps that would make it very difficult for him to master the profession. No memory to hold the books full of symptoms and remedies,— a patient might die while he was going back to the office to study up what was the matter.

"Which of these two men would have the best chance of success?"

"The first one."

"And which most closely resembles your own case?"

"The second."

"Do you really think, then, that you would have a good chance to make a success of the medical profession?"

"I don't know that I would. I never thought of it this way before, I just knew it was a good business, highly respected, and that's what I wanted."

"But there may be other highly respectable lines of work in which you would not be at so great a disadvantage.

116 CHOOSING A VOCATION

"Suppose a lot of races were to be run. In some of them you would have to run with a heavy iron ball tied round your leg, while others ran free. In other races you could run free as well as the rest of them, and have something like a fair chance. Which sort of race would you enter?"

"I'd rather run free, of course."

"Well, your hands appear to be just as good as anybody's. You can exercise care and industry. You can remember a few things, and can be successful if you don't attempt too much. If you go out into some sort of work where you won't have to meet so many people as a doctor must, nor remember such a vast mass of facts, — something where the memory and the personal element will not be such important factors, so that your handicap in these respects will not cripple you, — you may run the race on fairly equal terms and have a good chance of success. Some mechanical or manufacturing industry, wholesale trade where you would handle stock, care of poultry, sheep, cows, or other out-door work, would offer you good opportunities and be better for your health than the comparatively sedentary and irregular life of a physician.

"I suggest that you visit stock and dairy farms, carpenter shops, shoe factories, wholesale stores, etc., see a good many industries in the lines I have spoken of, read about them, talk with the workmen and managers, try your hand if you can at various sorts of work, and make up your mind if there is not some business that will interest you and offer you a fairly equal opportunity free from the special handicaps you would have to overcome in professional life."

The counselor also made specific suggestions about the cultivation of memory and manners, and a systematic course of reading and study to prepare for citizenship, and to develop economic power and social understanding and

SAMPLE CASES 117

usefulness, that would entitle the young man to the esteem of his fellow citizens.

As the youth rose to go he wiped his hand so it would be dry as he shook hands with some warmth and thanked the counselor for his suggestions, which he said he would try to follow. He smiled for the first time as he said this, and the counselor, noting it, said: —

"There! You can smile. You can light up your face if you choose. Now learn to do it often. Practice speaking before the glass, till you get your face so it will move and not stay in one position all the evening like a plaster mask. And try to stop saying 'Ss-uh.' When you want to say *Yes, sir,'* say it distinctly in a clear, manly tone, and not under your breath like a steam valve on an engine. A good many times when you say 'Ss-uh' it is n't necessary to say anything, and the rest of the time you should say 'Yes, sir,' or make some definite comment in a clear voice full of life and interest. Watch other people, and imitate those you admire, and avoid the things that repel or displease you in people you do not like."

"Ss-uh — yes, sir," said the boy, with another faint smile, "I'll try." And he was gone.

He told another young man a few days later that "the Professor" said he would go through him with a lantern, and he had certainly done it, and he was glad of it, for he learned more about himself that evening than in all his life before; and though part of it was like taking medicine at the time, it was all right, and he knew it would help him a great deal.

Case 12

FROM BOOTBLACKING TO SIGN PAINTING

Boy of nineteen; small, thin, weak; grammar-school education; very little reading; memory poor. His father

118 CHOOSING A VOCATION

drives an express wagon. Went to work at fourteen. Successively, office boy at $3 a week, florist's helper at $4.50 a week, and driver of delivery wagon for provision store at $5 and $6 a week. Got sick and lost his job. Went to work blacking boots at a stand in a billiard hall. Loves music and drawing. Spends spare time with pencil and cornet. Saved $63 to buy a silver cornet and $38 for lessons, while he was making $4.50 and $5 a week. Gave his mother half and saved the rest for cornet and lessons. Thought of studying to take civil service examinations for clerkship in post office.

Counselor asked him to bring some of his sketches. He did so. They showed considerable ability in outline work and lettering. Best points evidently in drawing and music.

Suggestions.

"If all the boys in Boston were to be divided into classes according to their special aptitudes and abilities, in what class would you belong? Is there anything you can do that most of the boys could not do so well?"

"Most of them cannot play the cornet, or draw as well as I can, I think."

"How would you like to use your ability for drawing and lettering by getting to be a sign painter?"

"I would like it very much."

"Well, practice a little every day or several times a day if possible. Watch the signs on the streets and copy the best ones. Study the advertisements in good magazines. Copy the lettering. Reproduce it from memory over and over again till you have mastered several good alphabets, plain and ornamental, and can use them at will in making signs and designs of your own. Borrow an engraver's book to get all the letters of each style in a complete group. When you have mastered a few kinds of letters so you can do plain and fancy lettering easily and rapidly, try to get a place in one of these sign-making shops and work up. If

SAMPLE CASES   119

you do well and save your money as you did for the cornet, you may be able in a few years to start a shop of your own. Don't drop your music; you may get into a band some day, though it is doubtful if you are strong enough to rely on that as a business."

Some weeks later the counselor met the young man in the subway. He had followed the suggestions made to him, had developed considerable skill and facility in lettering, got a place in an excellent shop, and was making signs to his heart's content. Had one of them with him on the way to delivery, a very creditable piece of work, and he was brimming over with enthusiasm and happiness, — did not seem like the same boy who had come a few weeks before to see how he could get a start.

Case 13

A GIFT FOR LANGUAGES

Young man of twenty; fine appearance; strong, athletic figure; handsome, expressive face; clear skin and eye; smiling, neat, manly, well-mannered, attractive in every way. Clean, intelligent, careful, social, free from bad habits except smoking before and after meals. Good-tempered, never had a fight or serious quarrel. Always been a leader among the boys; organized a number of clubs, and done a good deal of public speaking. Born in Russia. Went to Paris the next year. There eleven years, then came to Boston. Went to school in Paris, and two terms in Boston at the Phillips School. Best studies were arithmetic and languages, took several prizes. Poorest records in drawing and grammar. Has picked up a working knowledge of five languages. His father, a small merchant tailor, has a working knowledge of ten languages. The boy has read Victor Hugo's "Les Misérables" both in French and English; also fond of Shakespeare. Reads the

120 CHOOSING A VOCATION

editorials in the *Herald* and the *American*, also the general political news, but cares nothing for murder trials, divorce cases, or sporting news. Went to work at fourteen as a store boy at $2 a week. Worked five years in different dry goods and department stores as errand boy, stock boy, and salesman, getting $3.50, $4, $6, and $7 a week. Then got a place as a traveling salesman for a tobacco house, and made $13 or $14 a week. The firm transferred their business to a distant Western city. The boy wanted to stay with his people, so he did not go with the house. Said he had about concluded to take a civil service course and try to get into the post office as a clerk or a carrier, though he would rather be a traveling salesman if he could.

When the record, containing all this and a great deal more, was finished, the counselor said: —

"What are your distinguishing characteristics, the traits by which a naturalist might classify you?"

The boy hesitated.

"If all the young men in Boston were gathered here, in what respects, if any, would you excel most of them? In what respects would you be on a level with the rest, and in what respects, if any, would you be inferior?"

"I think most of the boys would not know so many languages, nor have done as much organizing or public speaking."

"Language, leadership, organizing ability, seem to be your distinguishing characteristics, the traits that would put you in a group with a small division of Boston's boys."

"Yes, I think that is so."

"Does a man win fame, position, money, success by the exercise of those faculties in respect to which he is specially strong, or by the exercise of faculties in respect to which he has only average ability or is inferior?"

"A man wins by his strong points, of course, not by his weak ones."

SAMPLE CASES   121

"Will your gifts for language, leadership, and organization come in play as a postal clerk, or will the boy without such abilities have about as good a chance in sorting letters or carrying the mail?"

"I might do something in the post office, perhaps, but it is plain enough that there are better fields for the sort of thing I can best do."

The counselor and the youth went over the list of industries together, and decided that teaching languages, translating, interpreting, political or social work among the immigrant populations of a large city, or work in a big mercantile house having correspondence and dealings with people of many nationalities, would offer the best opportunities for the full development and advantageous use of the young man's special abilities.

The first two lines of effort did not attract him, but any of the others he would like, especially civic or social work that would lead to public speaking and organizing, or a mercantile connection that would send him among different nationalities as a salesman or agent.

Methods were discussed and plans developed for more thorough preparation and for finding a good opening on the right line. One suggestion was that the youth should take one language after another and *perfect* his knowledge of it, *master* it; not merely read a little here and there in periodicals, as he had been doing, but make a systematic study of the grammar, read some of the best books in that language, and learn to write and speak it fluently. The counselor also suggested that smoking should be given up as a useless, expensive, and injurious habit. This suggestion did not meet with favor. But the young man expressed his gratitude for the light and inspiration that had come to him during the interview. He saw the path to his best usefulness and success clear before him. And he went away full of enthusiastic determination to take up

122   CHOOSING A VOCATION

Italian first, and afterward French, Spanish, etc., and turn his working knowledge into a mastery, in preparation for the opportunity that will surely come to put his best powers into practical use.

Case 14

A LAWYER IN THE MAKING

A bright boy of seventeen; German descent; ancestry distinguished and very well-off on both sides, but paternal grandfather lost his money (property confiscated by Russian government) and father has not recovered it. Twice set up in business by his father-in-law, but did not succeed in winning wealth.

The boy is one of the best, — high type in character and ability, fine looking, pleasant manners, good speaker, loves argument, greatly interested in public questions. Grammar school, two years of evening high, and three years of Breadwinners' Institute. Excellent records in all studies but drawing. President of class in grammar school. Read Scott, Dickens, Shakespeare, Cooper, Dumas. Very fond of books, dogs, horses, children, music, theatre, public meetings, discussions, etc. Memory good, analytic power excellent. Clear, forceful thinker, and tenacious debater. Careful, reliable, industrious, persistent, enthusiastic, open-minded, sympathetic, good-tempered, sociable. Free from bad habits, except a slight tendency to let his shoulders sag forward as he stands, and to converse at times without putting due life and emphasis into his voice. Walks ten miles or more at a stretch, but takes no other exercise. Salesman in dry-goods store, but does n't like trade. Wants to be a lawyer, and is willing to work hard to accomplish his purpose.

The counselor saw no occasion to discourage this ambition, but made some suggestions as to method.

SAMPLE CASES 123

1. Get Bigelow on Torts and analyze it. Reduce the substance of the first chapter to a single page of writing and bring it to me for criticism.

2. In the fall take the evening course at the Y. M. C. A.

3. Throw your shoulders back. Stand up straight.

4. Take more varied exercise. Bring the muscles of the body, arms, and neck into vigorous play with the punching bag or rowing or general gymnasium work. Breathe deeply in the open air. It is very important for one who is to work with his head to send strong currents of rich blood along the spine and through the head and into every part of the body.

5. Watch your voice. Put vitality and music into it even in ordinary conversation. Study the tunes of speech and use them.

The young man is reporting regularly, bringing in analyses of his legal reading, and most of them are very good indeed for a beginner. He enjoys the study greatly, and gets a good grip on the fundamentals.

Case 18

THE SECRET OF EFFECTIVE PREACHING

A fine-looking, healthy young man of twenty; bright, expressive face, engaging smile, pleasant manners, natural, cordial, and attractive; well-shaped head; memory rather poor; language fair; good habits; social, sympathetic, and inclined to look at life from the ethical standpoint. No specially weak points, or strong ones, either, except his pleasing appearance and address and his sympathetic disposition. Moderate education, grammar school in West Indies, leaving at the age of seventeen. Went to business college in Bellevue, Ontario, six months. No reading to speak of. Worked on farm two months; rest of time bookkeeping, receiving $11 a week. No manual or

124 CHOOSING A VOCATION

business skill or experience, nor any decided mental aptitudes, but decided aversion to mechanical, agricultural, or commercial lines. Had decided to go to college and prepare for Episcopal ministry. The college was determined upon, and the ultimate location, — his former home in the West Indies.

Excellent character, consecration to ethical ideals, attractive personality, a social and sympathetic temperament, and a spirit of genuine helpfulness are among the chief qualifications for a good pastor, and these were either possessed by the young man, or could be cultivated by him with good probability of success. Vocation fully determined upon, and choice apparently fairly well considered.

Suggestions, therefore, related mainly to methods of attaining the fullest fitness for the ministry, securing the best results as a pastor, and developing efficiency in the pulpit. Some of the suggestions were as follows: —

1. Cultivate memory. Was supplied with analysis of method of developing and using memory, with explanations and illustrations.

2. Study lives and work of great ministers, like Phillips Brooks, Henry Ward Beecher, and others, and try to discover the secrets of their success, — the essential respects in which they differed from the ordinary humdrum clergy man.

3. High character, broad sympathy, helpfulness, genuine service, love of humanity, devotion to high ideals, characterize the true preacher.

4. Knowledge of human nature, history, government, economics, public questions, is even more essential than knowledge of theology.

5. Learn to preach not only on Biblical matter, but on the problems that face men in daily life, and draw your illustrations of spiritual truth from concrete pictures of

SAMPLE CASES 125

life. The sermons of the best and most effective preachers always deal with *life*. They apply the principles of Christianity to daily affairs of business, politics, society, home, and individual life. No dry doctrinal sermons, but sermons brimful of light, sympathy, inspiration, and intelligent helpfulness in relation to the things that fill up the lives of the people; the right and wrong of industry and civic life in city, state, and nation, as well as the ethics of the home and private conduct.

All these things were preeminently true of Beecher and Brooks and other eminent clergymen of the past. Henry Ward Beecher used to say, "Christianity is not a doctrine but a life."

After listening to Phillips Brooks two or three times a week for six or eight months, I said to him, "Dr. Brooks, I've been trying to find out what it is that makes your sermons so attractive, and I've concluded that, aside from your captivating earnestness and literary power, the charm lies in the fact that you always make your thought touch daily life. You illumine common, every-day affairs with the light of Christian principle. You constantly apply ethical ideas and inspirations to life in all its phases, so that religion invades the week, stays with the people seven days instead of one, and goes with them into market, factory, street, court room and legislative hall; religion becomes a part of life instead of a thing more or less apart from life, a thing to put on once a week like your Sunday hat. That seems to me the secret, — your sermons deal with concrete daily life from the religious standpoint."

"Well," said the great divine, "what is preaching for but that?"

It is clear, then, that a first-class minister must know a great deal more than is taught in theological seminaries. He must be an all-round man.

126 CHOOSING A VOCATION

His field is the ethical and religious interpretation of life and the world, and ministration to the sympathies, ideals, and aspirations of his people.

To do his work properly, therefore, he must not only study ethics and religion, but must know life and the world, not only from books, but from personal contact and experience. Man, nature, industry, government, science, literature, and art all have a place in his equipment.

The world is hungry for ministers of a high type; men of light and sympathy and power, — men who know life as well as the history of the church, — men who can help the people solve the problems of daily life, as well as preach a funeral sermon or recite the catechism in sonorous tones.

Case 19

AN EMBRYO FORESTER

A vigorous young man of twenty-two; clerk in a small store, fairly successful, trusted by his employer with the general handling of the business and all the money that goes to the bank. But does not like commerce. Passionately fond of nature, — trees, grass, flowers; often walks out ten or fifteen miles to be in the woods, among the trees and out of the din and turmoil and deceit of the city. Grammar school, and five years evening study since. Head of his class in school, and has taken prizes for oratory. Careful, earnest, intelligent, and persistent.

"How would you like to be a florist, or study forestry and enter the Government service, which is being developed so rapidly now?" asked the counselor. "You might live with the trees then, and study them and care for them, as a gardener does with his roses or a dairyman with his cattle."

"That would suit me exactly. Do you think I can do it?

SAMPLE CASES   127

I will work very hard to do it, but I have to earn my living and help my family some for a year or two, till my brother and sister are able to support themselves."

"Are you willing to go West or South, or wherever the forest work may call you?"

"Yes, I'll go anywhere."

"Well, then, we'll do our best to fix it up together. And we can begin work right away. Go to the public library and make a list of what they have on forestry. Look over the more recent books, take out the one you think is the best, and I'll show you how to make an analysis of it and master the essential facts and principles. We'll also get the bulletins and lists of books and forestry schools from the Government Forest Service, collect a little library of the best books for systematic study, and correspond with the various schools and colleges to see if we can find a chance for you to earn some money while taking a course of forestry. Even if you don't find it right away, you will be practically free in a year or two, and meantime you can be studying treeology in the books and in the forest, and preparing yourself to make the most of your college course when the time comes."

This programme was begun at once, and is being systematically carried out to the budding forester's great delight. I have never seen a boy devour a science with more enthusiasm than this lover of trees displays in absorbing the principles and practice of forestry.

Case 22

A MECHANIC OFF THE TRACK

A young man of thirty; tall, fine-looking, well-built; clear, keen, fine expression; pleasant voice and manners; excellent conversational power; evidently a man of considerable culture and ability; bookkeeper for an advertis-

128   CHOOSING A VOCATION

ing concern, — fairly successful, making $25 a week; liked
the work, but not quite satisfied that he was in the right
line since hearing the counselor talk about the value of a
union of the best abilities and enthusiasms with the daily
work. He had a high-school education and course in a
business college, and had done some good reading on his
own initiative.

In answering such questions as: "How do you spend
your spare time?" "What sort of books do you like best?"
"If you were in a big library with plenty of time on your
hands, what department would attract you most?" "If you
were to visit the great expositions like the World's Fairs
at Chicago and St. Louis, where there were magnificent
buildings and beautiful grounds; a great collection of
manufactured products from all over the world; educational exhibits; military and naval exhibits; Machinery
Hall, full of all kinds of machinery; Transportation Building, full of locomotives, cars, carriages, automobiles, etc.;
Forestry, Agricultural and Mining buildings, crowded with
splendid exhibits in those lines; people from many different nations; wild animals; theatrical exhibits; curiosities
without number; what would you go to see first, what
would interest you most?" In answering all such questions, his love for machinery came strongly into view. He
spent his spare time with tools, making things or tinker-
ing about the house. His favorite reading consisted in
books about machinery. At the World's Fair he would go
first to Machinery Hall. That would interest him the most
of all. He had a passion for machinery. He loved to take it
apart and put it together again. He could understand a
new machine without instructions. He delighted to solve
mechanical problems.

In addition to his love of machinery and ability to
understand and handle it, he had strong analytic power,
which was clearly shown by a number of fine specimens of

SAMPLE CASES 129

his work exhibited to the counselor. His record and work also gave evidence of considerable inventiveness and organizing ability.

"Is there full scope in bookkeeping for the exercise of your best abilities, — your ability to deal with machinery, your analytic power and organizing ability?"

"No, there is n't."

"What lines of industry, then, would give full scope for your best powers?"

"Some mechanical work."

"Is not the question, then, what line of mechanical work offers you the best opportunities and fullest advantages?"

The young man thought this was so. We went over various mechanical industries together, and he decided to take a course in the Y. M. C. A. Automobile School and also a course in Electricity with a view to completing his studies in the Massachusetts Institute of Technology. Effort was also to be made at once to transfer his work in bookkeeping to some manufacturing company, where he would come into contact with machinery, and so help the change to mechanical activities.

At the end of the interview he shook the counselor's hand most heartily, and said he thought this had been the most important hour of his life, the most illuminating talk he had ever had. The conference, he believed, would change the whole course of his life.

If this young man had continued to be a bookkeeper for the rest of his life, his best powers and ambitions and enthusiasms would have been divorced from his daily work. He would have spent his working hours with the ledgers and account books and his spare time with machinery. By changing to a mechanical occupation he can unite his highest abilities and enthusiasms with his daily work, and so attain a development, success, and happiness that would otherwise have been impossible.

130 CHOOSING A VOCATION

The transfer to the employ of a company where he would come into contact with machinery was effected a few weeks after the interview.

Case 23

ARCHITECT OR PHYSICAL DIRECTOR

Young man of twenty-three; medium size, good-looking, clear complexion, athletic, extremely fond of physical exercise, very sociable nature, the human and social elements very strong; idealism and constructiveness much weaker, memory fair, manual ability medium; assistant physical director in a Y. M. C. A., and vibrating between the plan of perfecting himself for a full fledged physical directorship and the completion of his studies in architecture, a business he began to study and worked at for some time in an architect's office with fair results.

The counselor suggested that each should make a comparison of the two vocations in parallel columns, and then compare notes at a second interview. The following diagram gives the results: —

Physical Director.	*Architect.*
Active life.	More sedentary.
Healthful work.	Less healthful.
Close contact with men.	The human element much weaker and less constant.
Fine, helpful, sympathetic relationships.	Work more with things than with men; fair relationships but not so close, constant, or personally helpful.
The human element constant and strong.	More attention to drawings and buildings than to human beings as such.
Easy access — already have a good start in the profession	Idealism and constructiveness very important elements. Manual skill and mathematics and executive ability also.

SAMPLE CASES   131

Fair pay.	Large compensation if successful.
Little or no capital required.	No capital necessary if one works as an employee in an architect's office, But —
	Considerable capital is needed to establish one's self in an independent business, for an architect must often make expensive drawings and estimates and wait a long time for his pay.

On the basis of this comparative statement the counselor made the following suggestions: —

"Do you not think that, on the whole, your abilities and inclinations, especially your strong tendency to and marked ability for an active life full of the human element, adapt you much better to the life of a physical director than to that of an architect?

"Do you believe that you would be permanently satisfied with the comparatively sedentary life of an architect, dealing with paper, pencil and ink, brick and mortar, wood and iron, and all the details of designing and constructing buildings, with comparatively little of the human element?

"Could building houses of wood and stone ever be so attractive to you as building up fine human bodies of flesh and blood?

"The direction in which our main enthusiasms and abilities lie is the direction in which we are most likely to win marked success. If you had a specially fine opening in architecture and a much poorer one in the other calling that would make a change in the basis for decision which possibly might appeal to you, but at present your opportunities appear to be better in the line of the physical directorship.

132 CHOOSING A VOCATION

"If you decide on the basis of fullest adaptability, most congenial life, and best opportunity in favor of the physical directorship, I hope you will proceed with all your energy and enthusiasm to perfect yourself for that work. A medical course and a course in the Y. M. C. A. Training School at Springfield, Mass., would be especially valuable.

"If you decide in favor of architecture as your life work you might first take an evening course in this study, saving your money meanwhile so as to be able to complete your studies at Tech.

"In any case I hope you will not confine your studies to your vocation. There are other things in life besides earning a living. A man should study to be a good citizen and a well-rounded human being, as well as to be an efficient worker. And, in fact, a man cannot be a first-class worker unless he knows more than his work. A good architect must know more than architecture. An A 1 physical director must know more than athletics and medicine."

The young man said these suggestions made his case perfectly clear, the tabular contrast of the two professions being especially illuminating to him. He would not be satisfied to devote himself to things rather than to men.

Case 33

BUSINESS OR LAW; A HOUSE HALF BUILT

Assistant buyer in a department store; thinks he would like to be a lawyer; twenty-two years old; small, healthy; low forehead, narrow head not very well balanced, high cheek bones, coarse features but bright and expressive, pleasant smile; rapid utterance, not very clear; moderate and non-aggressive intellectually, but energetic and enthusiastic in performance. Has a high-school education. Was first rate in mathematics, but very poor in his-

SAMPLE CASES 133

tory, — just managed to pass. Memory not very good. Read some of Dickens, Kipling, and Shakespeare. No study of oratory. Done very little speaking. Not fond of argument. Mild disposition, not combative at all. Now taking evening course in law. Questions on his law work brought answers so confused as to show that he has no clear idea of the matters he has been over, — no grip on the law or the proper methods of studying it. He says he is fond of store work, pretty successful in it, and would like to develop into a full fledged buyer; but one of his friends was going to be a lawyer and proposed that he should become a lawyer, too.

When the record was finished the counselor said: —

"When a man has a house half built, in a good location, foundation laid and walls well up, nearly ready to put on the roof, is it wise to abandon the building, choose a new location, and begin another building from the foundation up, when there is no necessity for the change nor any good reason to believe the new building will be better or perhaps as good as the first one that is nearly finished? Is that a wise proceeding?"

"It don't look so."

"Well, is n't that about what you are thinking of doing? It would probably take you ten years to get as near to success in the law as you are now in business. Moreover, you have tried business, and you know you can be reasonably successful there, while it is not clear at all that you would be successful in the law. Your memory is not very good. Your ideas as to the law of torts, which you have studied, are very confused and inadequate. You are twenty-two years old, and have shown no aptitude in the line of public speaking, nor any appetite for the discussion of public questions, or argument of any kind. The law is a fighting profession on one side, and opens on political life on the other. You do not seem to be cut out for intellec-

134 CHOOSING A VOCATION

tual conflict, nor to have any special interest in public affairs, — no symptoms of a legal or civic mind. Study comes hard to you. A lawyer ought to master a library full of books. That would be very difficult for you. Moreover, the law is a crowded profession. It is hard to get a foothold even when you are well adapted to the work. You appear to be far better adapted to commercial life than the law. It would certainly take you many years to get as near to success in the law as you are now in commerce."

"It seems very clear to me now that you state the facts," said the young man. "It is strange I did n't see it before. It would take a long time in the law to get where I am now in business. I like the store, and might as well stick to it and work up."

"I think you are right," replied the counselor. "It will not hurt you to finish your evening course in law. It is an excellent culture study. You are a citizen as well as a worker, and you ought to know something about law and government and economics. Read Fiske, Ely, Dole, Bryce, Shaw, and other writers our 'civic suggestions' indicate, as you can get the time, and read systematically to understand and remember what you read. This analysis of memory method will help you develop your memory and get better results from it" (giving the young man the leaflet on memory, with a few moments' explanation and emphasis of the leading points).

"Study your stock. Get familiar with values. Practice several times a day, whenever you can get a few minutes, concealing labels and mixing the goods, and then naming quality and price by sight and touch. Carry samples in your pockets, and educate your fingers while traveling in the street cars. Keep on till you can tell the qualities and prices with quickness and certainty, — tell them in the dark. Master your trade. Get acquainted with buyers and learn the secrets of the business. We'll give you letters to

SAMPLE CASES 135

one or two of the best. Join one or more business organizations where you can come into association with the best men in your line, and cultivate them. Take a good trade journal and get the best books relating to your business, and study them till you know their substance by heart. Practice drawing your stock from memory till you can locate every bit of it with the pencil as fast as your fingers can move. Study style and novelties. Watch the market and try to anticipate it. Watch what other buyers are doing, and go them one better if you can. Above all, remember that the fundamental secret of success in your business is genuine service to the public."

Case 57

MORE STUDY AND EXPERIENCE NEEDED TO REACH DEFINITE CONCLUSION

A six footer, nineteen years old, weight 159. Born at Wellesley Hills. Fine physique. Health excellent. Lost no time by sickness last three years. Head large, splendidly shaped; 7⅜ hat. Good-looking, manners and voice o. k.; memory good; careful, intelligent, modest, no bad habits. Father a gardener; his father an engineer on a large estate in England. Very inventive and successful. Mother's father also an engineer.

Education, grammar school. Best studies drawing and history; high mark in drawing. Not good in mathematics.

Reading: Inventions, mechanical news, and ads in current magazines; a few novels, — "The Crisis," "That Lass o' Lowrie's," etc.

Spare time spent generally in reading, and lately two or three evenings a week in gymnasium.

At World's Fair would go first to Machinery Hall; chief interest would be there.

In list of industries, chiefly interested in "Skilled Mechanic," "Steam Railroad," "Inventor," "Architect."

136 CHOOSING A VOCATION

Experience: Worked some at gardening while at school. Left school at sixteen. Went to work as office boy $2.50 a week. Stayed three years, ending as shipping clerk and buyer of office supplies, $9 a week. Left to learn jewelry engraving. Studied seven weeks, and found it would take three or four years, so went and got work as chainman on an irrigation survey, $30 a month and board. Winter came and work stopped. Last fall, 1907, went to Los Angeles, California. Had saved enough to pay fare and some over. No work in Los Angeles. Father sent money for ticket home.

Now working at bookkeeping in an insurance office, $8 a week. Did not study bookkeeping, just picked it up.

Comments and Suggestions.

Strong in drawing; loves machinery, reads about it, likes to see and handle it. Heredity points the same way. Ancestors — engineers on both sides, and one of them very inventive.

Mechanical mind and interest. Suggest skilled artisan, machinist, or engineer, in order to unite best ability and enthusiasm with daily work.

Read Fowler's "Starting in Life," and the books on our select list relating to modern mechanism and the history of invention. Visit various mechanical industries, railroad shops, machine shops, electrical works, shoe factories, foundries, watch factories, engine works, etc. See the men at work. Talk with them. Try your hand at the work if you can. When you have gained a close acquaintance with some of the principal lines of mechanical work by observation, reading, and experience, come back and we will go over the courses that are available in or near Boston for day or evening study and practice, in preparation for the mechanical business that may then seem best for you.

While studying out your vocation read for citizenship

SAMPLE CASES 137

and general culture, taking some of the books on the sheet of Civic Suggestions. It would be a good plan for you, perhaps, to begin with Fiske and Dole, following them with Forman, Bryce, and Bridgman.

The more the young man studied and investigated himself and his industrial problem, the clearer and stronger became the tendency to mechanical work; and as this statement is issued, word comes from him that he has accepted an opportunity to work his way through the Automobile School of the Boston Y. M. C. A., which offers a very thorough and practical course.

Case 64

MINING ENGINEER OR TEACHER AND ACCOUNTANT

Boy of nineteen; height 5 ft. ½ in., weight 137; well-built and handsome; winning smile and pleasant manners, well-shaped head, vigorous health. Has not lost two weeks in sickness in as many years.

Father a machinist. His father a tin peddler.

Education: Grammar and one year high; two years bookkeeping and shorthand; began railroad engineering course, International Correspondence School, but did not finish. All studies came easily; best records in mathematics, worst in spelling.

Reading: Cooper, Henty, Eliot, Scott, "Comedy of Errors," "Julius Caesar," etc. Not much reading in the last three years, so busy with work and study.

Experience: Went to work at fourteen in vacation time. Worked in shoe factory helping father at $10 a week. Father paid more than work was worth. Saved my money, bought my own bicycle, etc. In 1904 went to work steadily for the shoe company at $10 a week. In August, 1904, went to Brazil and Buenos Ayres with father. Worked there nine months teaching natives how to operate shoe machines at $10 and expenses. April, 1905, came back to

138   CHOOSING A VOCATION

Boston, went to Bryant & Stratton's, spending summer vacations in factory. In 1907 left school and went to work as bookkeeper and stenographer with a manufacturing firm at $10 a week. November, 1907, employed by an auditor, Professor ———, of the ——— School, to go to New York to audit the books of the F. D. Co., $15 a week and expenses. Afterward audited books of B. F. Co. of Boston for Professor ———, on the same terms. "Like the work very much; best job I ever had. Don't like the routine of steady bookkeeping, but auditing a set of books is fine."

"Was your work satisfactory to Professor ———?"

"Yes, he was pleased with the work we did." "What did he get from the company for the job?" "He got $700 from the New York company, and employed two of us boys to check up the books."

"What did it cost him for your pay and expenses?" "We worked about four weeks and a half. Our pay came to about $135, and expenses for both of us about $75."

"How much time did the auditor, Professor ———, put in on the job?"

"About ten days, I think."

"He got, then, something like $500 for ten days' work and his responsibility; about $50 a day, which is the sort of pay a first-class auditor can make. If you persevere until you qualify yourself to take the contract instead of being employed as a helper, you can multiply the $15 a week you have been getting by ten or twenty."

January, 1908, went to ——— Academy and started to prepare for Tech. Left in one week, found they did not give the right course to fit a man for Tech. Then went to Chauncy Hall School to prepare to enter Tech in the Mining Engineering Course. Doing stenographic work, and teaching two evenings in the ——— School, bookkeeping, commercial arithmetic, correspondence, and penmanship.

SAMPLE CASES 139

Likes teaching very much and is successful with the boys, and highly commended by the head of the school.

"How long would it take to perfect yourself to pass the state examination and become a certified accountant?"

"A year or so, perhaps; do not know exactly."

"How long would it take for you to go through the Engineering Course in the Institute of Technology?"

"Six years."

"What do you know about mining engineering? Have you ever visited a mine, or been acquainted with a mining engineer?"

"No."

"It seems that you have two good ways of earning money, one is teaching commercial subjects and the other is bookkeeping and accounting. Why should you not aim to become a teacher in a business high school or college, and take jobs of auditing as your Professor ———— does now? Or, you could soon become a certified public accountant, and devote yourself entirely to that sort of work.

"As a teacher of business subjects you could probably command in a few years from $1500 to $3000 a year, and there is a great demand for such teachers. As a public accountant you might hope to grow to an income of any-where from $5000 to $15,000 a year. You are planning to leave your work, which you know all about and thoroughly like, in which you have proved very efficient and satisfactory, and which holds out a promise of excellent remuneration with a little persevering effort on your part, — you are planning to leave all this to devote six years of study to preparation for a new line of work, about which you say you know practically nothing. Is it wise to spend all the time and money involved in this plan, without first investigating the business of mining engineering sufficiently to be sure that you would like the work better than auditing or teaching, and so have a solid basis for deciding that you had better leave teaching or auditing

140 CHOOSING A VOCATION

for the life of an engineer? The question of ability does not rise in this case, for you undoubtedly have the ability to fit yourself for an engineer if you conclude that that is the wise thing to do; but you have spent some of your best years in preparation for auditing and business teaching, and your preparation and experience in these lines should not be abandoned without excellent reason. You are practically ready to put the roof on the house you have been building. Don't leave it to begin a new structure from the ground up, unless you are sure that the new building will be enough better than the one you have now in process of construction to pay you for the sacrifice of time and effort that will be necessary to make the change.

"Make a diagram presenting a comparative study somewhat as follows; and then come back for another talk."

DIAGRAM	CERTIFIED PUBLIC ACCOUNTANT	TEACHER IN BUSINESS COLLEGE OR SCHOOL OF COMMERCE, WITH AUDITING CONTRACTS ON THE SIDE	MINING ENGINEER
How long will it take to complete your preparation?			
Cost of preparation.			
Opportunities and readiness with which you can get into the work.			
Pay, immediate, prospective.			
Conditions of work: Location. Kind of life. Human element. Healthfulness, etc.			
Other elements: Degree of independence. Social consideration. Satisfaction in the work. Its general nature and results, permanence, quality, importance.			

SAMPLE CASES 141

Case 70

BARRED BY THE PREJUDICE AGAINST AGE

A well-built man of fifty-nine, with white hair and mustache; troubled somewhat with rheumatism in his wrist, but otherwise quite vigorous and able. Was traveling salesman twenty-five years for a Boston wholesale drug and paint house, till the firm went out of business. Then sold in New England territory for the Buffalo linseed oil people a year and a half. Made excellent sales. Has sold as high as two hundred thousand dollars worth of goods in a year. Oil people found they could get along with one less man in Buffalo, so dismissed their new salesman and transferred to New England the spare man from Buffalo who had been with them a long time.

Been out of work now one year and five months. Has made many efforts to get employment. Sometimes the managers say they will give him work when they have a place, and then they hire younger men. Often the managers say they are limited to men under thirty-five, men who will grow up with the business and be good for many years.

Aged mother to support and savings almost exhausted. Completely discouraged, and shows it in face, voice, manner, and attitude.

Suggestions.

Rejuvenate yourself so far as possible. Pay strict attention to your personal appearance. Do not advertise your age, but advertise your strength. Be as young as possible. Put vim into your manner and voice. Put vitality into your tones and life into your face. So long as a man has vigor, age is largely a matter of mental attitude and will power. As Oliver Wendell Holmes used to say, it is better to be seventy years young than seventy years old.

Brace up. No one wants a man who acknowledges him-

142 CHOOSING A VOCATION

self as a down-and-out, a man who is defeated and discouraged and shows it. You are an experienced salesman. You know how to smile and tell a good story and talk up the goods you have to sell. You have some valuable labor to sell. The next time you try to dispose of it, don't tell a sad story or look like a funeral procession, but smile at the man; tell him your record for big sales, show him your recommendations, crack a joke with him, and talk as you used to talk when you were selling thousands of dollars worth a week. Talk as if you were making a fifty-thousand-dollar sale, and expected to win out. In other words, show your power in your application, and give the impression of strength and confidence.

You are a salesman, and a good one. What you need is not a new vocation, but work to do. Make a systematic canvas for work through your old friends, the men to whom you used to sell goods.

Do your best; and if it does n't work, come back and we'll see what more can be done to help you get a chance to use your experience and ability and make a living for yourself and your mother.

Case 72

TO BE OR NOT TO BE A STENOGRAPHER

Young man of twenty-seven; good-looking, pleasant voice and manners, cordial smile, very attractive presence. Health excellent, lost no time by sickness in the last five years; never was sick in bed. Born in Cambridge. Father a Methodist minister and ex-president of ———— University. Grandfather also a Methodist preacher. Great-grandfather a merchant and local preacher. Mother taught school. Her father and grandfather were Massachusetts farmers. Uncle on mother's side formerly owned a grocery, now traveling for the ———— Bible Society. One sister teaching;

SAMPLE CASES   143

another, a graduate of Simmons College, is secretary to a professor in a Western college. Older brother submaster in the ———— School. Three younger brothers in high school.

Education: Boston grammar and two years in Latin school; Mt. Hermon School three and one half years; and graduated B. S. from Wesleyan University, 1906. Best marks in algebra and arithmetic, sometimes top-notch. But liked modern languages and science best, especially chemistry. Ranked above the average, but no prizes.

Spends spare time in library, reading fiction, politics, and college sporting news, or in gymnasium. Theatre now and then; fond of Shakespearean plays and plays like "The Man of the Hour." Does n't care for musical comedy, or for music, or art. Has done no public speaking to amount to anything.

Worked in dry-goods store, in charge of stock. Later a service inspector for Telephone Company. Now in Y. M. C. A. office work. Thinking of teaching, or stenography.

Auditory reactions slow. Impressions quite imperfect. Verbal memory tests gave very poor results; could not repeat correctly easy sentences of twelve or fifteen words, even when read quite slowly and distinctly.

Suggestions.

To make an expert stenographer one should have a keen and accurate auditory memory, and capacity for rapid transfer of auditory and visual impressions from the brain through the hand. You are not quick, and your word memory is very poor. You might overcome these handicaps and become a fair stenographer, but your natural aptitudes do not seem to lie in that direction. The family drift appears to be toward teaching and the ministry, which is a combination of teaching and social work. Your record in school and college indicates that you might, perhaps, teach some branch of science or mathematics with credit

144 CHOOSING A VOCATION

and success. And your pleasing way of meeting people is an element of adaptation to Y. M. C. A. work or social work, teaching, or any business or profession which brings one into contact with many people.

You have devoted your life so far too much to books and too little to doing useful work. Acquiring knowledge is all right, but you should learn to use your knowledge also. Devote yourself to that as systematically as you did to acquiring knowledge in your college days.

If you feel strongly drawn to secretarial work, or have a specially good opportunity in that line, it may be well to go to a skillful and disinterested teacher of stenography and get him to test you long enough and thoroughly enough to make it quite clear whether it is worth while for you to pursue that line or not. My impression on the facts before us is that you would have a much better chance to make a good success in some educational line, or in general Y. M. C. A. work or social work. You might fit yourself probably for any one of many occupations, agricultural, mechanical, commercial, etc.; but your strong points now appear to be your pleasing address and your mathematical bent, and your weakest point appears to be your verbal memory, so that stenography is probably one of the callings for which you are not naturally well adapted.

Case 84

CONGENIAL WORK WITH DUE CARE FOR THE HEALTH

A fine girl of eighteen, beautiful and cultured, 5 ft. 6, and 140 lbs. A charming girl, of excellent family. Father a man of the finest type of character and ability. Head well shaped on the whole, but curves not full above the temples. Strong and well except that the nerves are not in perfect tone. Trouble with nerves for several years,

SAMPLE CASES

145

brought on by overstudy. Could not concentrate. Had to stay out of high school a year. Has to be careful still; can't concentrate fully. Verbal memory quite imperfect both on visual and auditory tests.

In third year of high school. Last year got A's in everything the whole year through. This year A's and B's mixed. Likes algebra, geometry, physics, history, English composition, and gymnasium work best; foreign languages least. Read Kipling's "Jungle Stories," Morgan's "Somehow Good," and a lot of stories. Careful, coöperative, reliable, earnest; will-power and perseverance excellent.

Would like to do something, something besides housework; likes housework when working with others, but wants to do something in the world. Went through the list of industries open to women, stating which were attractive and which were to be regarded as very undesirable for her. Results as follows: —

Would like,	*Would not like,*
(A) Journalism. "Nothing I'd like better, — not writing fiction but facts."	Care of animals or plant culture. Making food products or textile manufactures, selling goods. Domestic work.
(A) Social or Welfare work — helping to manage to operate a college settlement, for example, or a department of it, or other work of social value. Teaching physical culture.	Hotel or restaurant. Home manufactures. Commercial callings, agencies, teaching library work, law, medicine, surgery, artistic group or employments
(A) Secretarial work. Might be willing to do office work or take civil service position; but would not care specially for it.	

The three occupations marked (A) were the most attractive in our list of over two hundred ways in which women are earning money.

Suggestions.

1. Interests may change as experience broadens and deepens. Five years from now you may be as thoroughly interested in homekeeping as you are now in writing and social work. But meantime, while you are developing and getting a fuller and more varied knowledge of life and industry, we can test your abilities and your present interests (which seem to be fairly well founded and in line with the indications of heredity and family environment), to see if the best of both can be united with your daily work at the same time that due respect is paid to your health.

2. You should be careful not to engage in work that is very confining and sedentary, or involves any serious strain on the nervous system. Health is the first point. Your work should, if possible, be such as to help the nerves and heart and build up strength rather than make large demands on nervous power, at least for a few years. Your memory trouble and difficulty in concentration apparently have their source in lack of physical tone, and are probably only temporary, but must be allowed for at present.

Secretarial work is confining, and may make considerable demands on memory and concentration. Moreover the worker is at the call of the employer, who may need to make the largest demands at a time when the worker is ¹ ˑt fitted to bear the strain.

Your memory handicap also points against secretar-
A stenographer should have a good verbal mem-
ˑndicap in relation to authorship or journalism
ˑ great, though still of some weight. I shall
ˑvsis of the methods of cultivating the

SAMPLE CASES

147

memory and getting the best results from it, which will help you to overcome your difficulty in this respect.

4. I do not find in your case the strenuous appetite for reading on the line of the literary talent or ambition, or the spontaneous overflow into MSS. or expression of some kind that is usually manifested by those who are specially adapted to authorship.

This is only a straw, by no means conclusive. Heredity points the other way, and some of the best writers have developed the gift of expression pretty late in life.

5. Social work in many lines is less confining and puts less strain on memory, concentration, etc. Active social or welfare work under good conditions helps the health, and brings the best powers and enthusiasms into play. You have an excellent opportunity for training in this direction and easy access to such work, through your father's skill, reputation, position, and associations. And you could unite it with writing or journalism, — social work naturally flows to such expression, — unite it with writing easily and effectively, without the risk of the over-confinement and nervous strain incident to a life entirely devoted to authorship or journalism.

6. Please bring me some of your compositions.

7. Make a full blue book study of yourself in answer to the questions on this sheet of " Personal Data," and then come for another consultation.

8. Read "Careers for Women" and the relevant parts of Fowler's "Starting in Life," and see as much as you can of different industries.

9. Read, think, talk, cultivate thoughtful people; watch the inner light, note the things that interest you most, tell them to your friends, write about them, take the MS. to some accomplished writer for criticism, compare it carefully with the best writings in its class; and when revised, invigorated, and polished to the best of your abil-

148 CHOOSING A VOCATION

ity, send it to some magazine or newspaper. If the MS. comes back to you send it to another publication, and keep on till you get it published or are pretty sure you can't get a publisher. Do this with one article a month at first, and as you gain facility make it one short article a week at least.

10. It would be well to take your subjects, in part at least, from your own actual experiences in social work. That will unite your two chief interests in work that can be made consistent with care for your health, and in a way that will be helpful to both interests. The fact that you are going to write about your social work will give it additional interest and vigor; and the fact that your writing is carved out of personal experience will help to give it strength and vitality.

The Chelsea relief work offers you fine opportunities just now for vital experiences in helping the sufferers solve their problems.

11. Study Irving's "Sketch-Book," Kipling's "Plain Tales," Jack London's books, Jacob Riis's "Battle with the Slum" and "How the Other Half Lives," "Mrs. Wiggs," "Timothy's Quest," "Patsy," "Sesame and Lilies," "Crown of Wild Olive," "Rab and His Friends," "A-Hunting of the Deer," "Birds and Bees," "Wild Animals I Have Known," "The Bonnie Brier Bush," Emerson's Essays and Bacon's, Shakespeare's Plays and Sheridan's, "The Light of Asia," "Letters from a Chinese Official," Omar's "Rubaiyát," and Wendell Phillips's Speeches, to help you acquire vividness, condensation, unity, imagery, and humor, and develop a clear, strong, picturesque, and popular style.

12. Practice writing a little every day. Intervals of length hinder or arrest development. It is frequent effort that produces rapid growth of facility and power.

If you follow these methods with persistent industry for a year or so, you cannot fail to be greatly benefited,

SAMPLE CASES   149

and your possibilities in the directions indicated will probably become so clear as to make it easy for you to form a
definite conclusion in the matter.

Since the interview this young lady has entered the
regular college course in preparation for journalism in the
University of Wisconsin.

Case 88

A FARMER'S BOY IN THE CITY

A tall, strong, good-looking boy of eighteen; pleasant
mannered, soft-spoken, intelligent, modest, retiring.
Brought up on his father's farm. Health perfect; never
sick as far back as can remember. Lost fingers of left hand
in trolley accident. Educated in country grammar and
high schools. Best records in stenography, commercial
geography and arithmetic, algebra and English history;
poorest in American history (because of the use of the
research method in that study) and in English. No reading of much account. Does n't like farm work except the
care of animals. Left farm little over year ago. Worked a
month as stenographer in business house at $8 and $10 a
week. Since then he has been doing general office and
clerical work in a public institution at $8 a week. Spends
two evenings a week taking a course in stenography. Says
he has made speeds of 100 to 130 words a minute in
school dictation. But speed is helped by familiarity with
the routine of business correspondence used for school
dictation. My test with plain, simple English statement of
matter unfamiliar to him gave 65 words a minute.
Auditory memory fair when using simple sentences he
could easily understand; but very poor when using sentences from Emerson's Essays, the meaning of which he
did not readily grasp. Spends spare time walking about
the streets or sitting on the steps with other young fel-

150 CHOOSING A VOCATION

lows, just having a social time. Does not belong to any organizations except the Y. M. C. A. Has made no plans beyond a course in stenography and one, perhaps, in bookkeeping. A friend connected with the school where he is taking stenography advised him to consult the Vocation Bureau, so he came to see the counselor.

Comments and Suggestions.

"It is surely time you began to work out a definite plan of life. You are just drifting now in a little boat, without compass or chart. You cannot expect to make a good voyage or reach an important port that way.

"You want to develop your economic value, and your civic and social value also. You want to increase your earning power and get the money. And you also want to make yourself a good citizen and valuable member of society so that you will deserve the respect of your fellow men. Is n't that so?"

"Yes."

"Well, you are not moving in that direction very rapidly now, are you?"

"No."

"You are just vegetating; living like one of the big elms on your father's farm, or one of his horses; following the ordinary routine of life, without thought for the future, — leaving the thinking and planning to others, who are therefore making all the money.

"You do not want to be simply a machine, to transform the energy in a certain amount of food each day into typewriting or clerical work. You know practically nothing about what is going on in the world, nothing of the great movements of the age in which you live, nothing of science or literature. In the same building, and on the same floor with the office in which you work, is a library that contains many of the world's best books. If Shakespeare,

SAMPLE CASES 151

or Emerson, or Ruskin, or Wendell Phillips should come to speak in Boston you would want to hear the address, would n't you?"

"Yes."

"And if you could have such men for your daily companions you would think yourself highly privileged?"

"Yes, I would."

"Well, there they are across the hall from you, waiting to speak to you and give you their companionship. They have put the best of themselves into their books, and it is all yours for the asking.

"A cow may be excused for grazing placidly over a gold mine and never attempting to get at the precious metal that is so near her; but a *man* ought not to behave in that way."

(These remarks, seasoned with sympathy and interest evident in tone and smile and cordial manner, did not displease the young man, but quite the contrary.)

"You will soon be one of the rulers of the United States, and one of the directors of the corporation of Boston and the State of Massachusetts, responsible for your proper share in the government of city, state, and nation. What are you doing to fit yourself for the trust? Practically nothing. Yet I'm sure you want to fit yourself for that great trust to the best of your ability. Is n't it so?"

"Yes" (heartily).

"Well, this sheet of Civic Suggestions, and some of the books I have marked for you to read, will help you.

"You want to develop a full, well-balanced manhood. Making a living is only one arc of the circle. You must be a good citizen as well as a good worker. You don't want to be alive only on one side, and dead on the other.

"Coming back to your work: It is not clear at all that stenography is the right thing for you. You are not spe-

152 CHOOSING A VOCATION

cially quick, nor gifted with auditory retentiveness. You are weak in English and general information. You don't love the work, or you would devote more energy to it than a little time two evenings a week. You look at it simply as a means of earning a living. Your heart is not in it. Stenography is a poor field for a man unless he is going to be a gilt-edged expert, and at best there are fewer prizes than in agriculture, stock raising, manufactures, commerce, etc.

"You may make a good office hand or private secretary, or even an expert perhaps, if you will practice constantly enough to get the thing into your blood and make it automatic or reflex, and will get a thorough knowledge of the English language and a fair understanding of men and affairs as well as speed and accuracy as a stenographer and typewriter. A first-class stenographer must have more than double your speed, and must have enough general knowledge to understand the sense of the matter he writes and the work he is called on to do. He must know the English language as well as the keyboard of his typewriter.

"But the possibilities even at the top are not very large, while the great pressure of feminine competition in all the lower and middle strata of the business makes it undesirable for a man of moderate skill, who must earn enough to support a family. A man may make a good income from stenography if he is rapid enough to be a court stenographer (but the work is a severe strain on the nervous system), or if he can build up a school of stenography, or can secure enough business to employ a number of girls and get for himself the manager's pay and employer's profits, or if he can combine his stenographic skill with other abilities sufficient to give him a good position as private secretary to some business man, public official, or literary worker.

SAMPLE CASES 153

"You like the care of animals, you say. Raising poultry, dogs, sheep, horses, etc., market gardening, fruit raising, flower culture, etc., offer a man like you more chance for income, independence, and social position, than stenography, besides being much more healthful and in line with the bulk of your experience, so that the maximum use of your past life would be available.

"Agricultural pursuits, when mixed with brains and science, mean prosperity and happiness. It is only when divorced from science that they lose their interest and become drudgery.

"You have youth and health and a fairly good head. Enthusiasm and persistent industry will do the rest.

"But the fact is, that you have not yet had sufficient experience to develop your interests and aptitudes. You know very little about yourself or about the world."

"That is true."

"You do not understand either well enough to form a good basis for conclusion as to the true relation between the two. You must study yourself and study the world, in order to be able to decide what you are best fitted to do, and how you can unite the best of yourself with your daily work. The great thing now in this relation is to focus your mind on the problem. Visit the Agricultural College at Amherst if possible, and by all means read about Luther Burbank's wonderful experiments in creating new varieties of fruits and flowers almost at will."

Case 90

I DON'T SEE ANY FUTURE IN MY WORK

A man of thirty-eight; unmarried; tall, well-built, good-looking; quiet, pleasing manners; good memory, clear head, careful, accurate, moderate initiative. Health excellent; does n't remember when he was sick; has n't missed

154 CHOOSING A VOCATION

a day from work on account of sickness for fifteen years, at least. Born and brought up in Boston; father was a salesman. Boy went to kindergarten, grammar, and high schools, and took two years special work in chemistry at the Massachusetts Institute of Technology. Circumstances made it necessary for him to go to work, and he left Tech before completing his course.

Began as errand boy for an iron house, $3 a week; stayed with the firm three years, working his way into the bookkeeping department at $9 a week. Left to take a place at $10 a week with a bag-making company. Been with the company ever since. Fifteen years of steady service; now has full charge of the books and a salary of $140 a month.

"Did the company raise your pay from time to time voluntarily, or did you have to ask for the increase each time?"

"I never asked for a raise. Every advance of pay was on my employers' own motion."

"Do you like bookkeeping?"

"Yes."

"You like the work and you are making $140 a month. What is the trouble?"

"I don't see any future in my work. I've got as high as I can where I am, and I don't want to stop at $140 a month. I want something ahead of me to work up to."

"Do you save your money?"

"Yes."

"And invest it?"

"Yes."

"Then you have one means of steady progress at least. And there are other methods you can readily apply.

"You have had over fifteen years' experience in bookkeeping and have been successful, as is shown by the fact that your employers have voluntarily lifted your pay from

SAMPLE CASES

155

$9 to $35 a week. You like the work, your only objection being that you can't see any future to it.

"Now, as a matter of fact, a thoroughly equipped accountant can make from $15 to $50 a day. The Civic Federation Commission, of which I was a member, paid its expert accountants $20 a day and expenses, and I know accountants who make $50 a day auditing sets of books for business houses, cities, etc."

"I had no idea the pay ran so high."

"If you felt that you were working toward a possible $20 or $30 a day, you would think there was future enough in your line of business to make you satisfied to continue in it and justify any reasonable amount of effort in self-development, would n't you?"

"Yes, I certainly would."

"Well, the prizes are there, and you can try for them. You are not more than a third of the way up the ladder in your profession. You have health and strength and ambition to help you climb higher up. Good certified accountants make $1500 to $3000 a year, even as salaried employees; and when a man acquires experience and acquaintance enough to work up a good business of his own or become a partner in a firm employing a corps of assistants, he may build up an income of $5000 or $6000 or even $10,000 in a city like Boston, and $15,000, $20,000, even $50,000 to $100,000 in New York, I am told. In fact, accountants tell me there is practically no limit to the income a first-class man can attain in New York as a member of an accounting house or partnership, if he thoroughly understands business affairs as well as accounting and has acquired large experience and acquaintance.

"Even in straight bookkeeping you have by no means reached the limit. You do not have to stay all your life in the place you are in. If you fit yourself for a larger field, you may get a place in a much larger house, where you

156 CHOOSING A VOCATION

will have a chance to work up to the head of the book-keeping department, with a body of workers under you and a salary two or three times as large as you have now.

"There is plenty of future in your line if you will work for it. I suggest that you ascertain the requirements for the State Examinations that must be passed in order to become a certified public accountant. We have no law of this kind yet in Massachusetts. But you can take the examination, and get your certificate in Rhode Island, or in New York.

"The evening courses in the Y. M. C. A. or Comer's Commercial School, or the day courses at Bryant & Stratton's, offer you the means of perfecting your knowledge of accounting and business finance. At Comer's you can begin right away and study all summer, if you choose.

"It is not necessary to wait till you get your certificate before pushing for a place in a larger house. You can begin a campaign for a wider field at once, in the way already suggested. Get an advertising expert to help you draw up the statement you place with the employment agencies, and watch the want ads for high-class book-keepers on your own account, apply in person for openings that attract you, and have a clear, concise, and well-worded statement of your record and experience that you can leave with the Employment Manager after you have talked with him, or send to him when you ask for an interview.

"Your progress depends: first, on perfecting your equipment, — developing your economic value by persistent, well-directed study for the purpose of mastering your profession; and second, on getting an opportunity to use your knowledge in a larger field, either as a public accountant or in the bookkeeping department of a bigger company. You must get the goods and take them to market. You must have what people want, and you must let

SAMPLE CASES 157

them know that you have it; those are the two main elements in such a case."

The young man entered into the plan with interest and enthusiasm. He saw the way to advancement clear before him, and said he would begin to work at once on the lines suggested by the counselor.

CASE INCIDENTS

Incidental suggestions often occupy an important part in the consultation. For instance, a boy who stammered two or three times during the interview was sent to the Stammerers' Institute, for the simple and effective treatment which is almost certain to cure him. A young man who seemed to be very bright and thoroughly competent, complained that he could not get on, could not secure advancement or any satisfactory reason why he was not advanced. The counselor called his attention to the fact that his voice in conversation was lifeless and unpleasant, — entirely below the standard he attained in other respects, and giving a decided impression, not only of lack of vigor and interest, but of want of intelligence. The youth believed he had found the key to his trouble, and reported some time later that the change in his ability to interest people and deal with them successfully was astonishing.

A young man of marked ability, who was quite clearly in the right line, but was with a house too small to admit of much advancement, and did not know how to get into a larger field, was advised to join a club where he would come in touch with the best business men of the city, and also to avail himself of the services of the best agencies for securing the class of work he was qualified to do.

In another case the usual inquiries in regard to saving and spending money brought out the fact that the boy wanted very much to get on in the world, but was discouraged about himself because he constantly let his money slip from him in dissipation. He was alone in the city, and when evening came he was lonesome, and he would drift into the theatre or some worse place nearly every night, and his money would go. The counselor suggested that he should join a boys' club, take up some evening studies that would bring him every night to the Civic Service House, and make a daily report in writing to the counselor or some one else he might select as a sort of trustee, showing just how much money he had spent in the last twenty-four hours and what he had spent it for. In a little while, if he did this faithfully, new interests and better habits would be formed, and he would become strong enough to live rightly without a guardian. He grasped eagerly at the chance of getting out of the mire, and put the method suggested in practice at once, with excellent results.

A Scotch-American boy at the second interview seemed listless and inert. On inquiry it appeared that he was troubled with constipation, and drugs did not seem to give him any permanent relief. The counselor gave him a memorandum of some simple hygienic remedies through diet, exercise, kneading, bathing, etc., and two weeks later he came back as bright as a new dollar, to say that one of the simplest of the methods suggested had fixed him all right. This may seem a little aside from the functions of a vocation bureau; but when it is considered that health is the foundation of industrial efficiency, that constipation, with the auto-poisoning that may follow, is a serious handicap, and that very few doctors will apply the simple remedies which are really most effective and beneficial, it is clear that such suggestions are not out of order in the work of helping young men to achieve efficiency and success.

The discussion of special cases could be continued almost indefinitely; but enough has been said to give some

SAMPLE CASES 159

notion of the work that is being done, and its possibilities for the future. The Civic Suggestions, the library work with its analytic reading and research, and the tabulated courses of study often create an interest that brings the young man back to the counselor again and again for brief reports or consultations.

XVI

CONCLUSIONS

THE work is constantly growing in extent and utility, but it must always be very inadequate as compared to the need, until it becomes a public institution affiliated or incorporated with the public-school system. This we hope will ultimately come to pass, as public education is extended and perfected and industrial training is developed.

Society is very short-sighted as yet in its attitude towards the development of its human resources. It trains its horses, as a rule, better than its men. It spends unlimited money to perfect the inanimate machinery of production, but pays very little attention to the business of perfecting the human machinery, though it is by far the most important in production.

Less than one sixteenth of the children in Boston primaries go through a high-school course. In Philadelphia less than one thirtieth of the children go through the high school, and in Washington less than one thirteenth.

Here are the data for these three cities, obtained at the opening of this year. The high-school figures include the pupils in all the schools and courses of high-school grade, commercial and manual training, as well as academic: —

PUPILS IN THE PUBLIC SCHOOLS

	BOSTON	PHILADELPHIA	WASHINGTON
First year primaries.	13,622	33,588	9,198
First year grammar.	10,007	19,386	5,601
Last year grammar.	4,869	5,710	3,136
Last year high schools.	850	1,089	663

CONCLUSIONS 161

Nearly two thirds of the children in Boston and Washington and five sixths in Philadelphia drop out of school even before they finish the grammar grades. There are not seats enough in the grammar schools, probably, for more than one tenth of the whole number. Our cities evidently do not expect or intend to educate the bulk of the boys and girls beyond the primaries or lower grammar grades. The mass of children go to work to earn their living as soon as they are old enough to meet the law, and often before that.

Science declares that specialization in early years in place of all-round culture is disastrous both to the individual and to society. There is a clear relation between intelligence and variety of action and experience. A knowledge of each of the great classes of industry by practical contact is the right of every boy. This varied experience should be obtained under a thoroughgoing scientific plan of educational development, and not by the wasteful and imperfect method of drifting from one employment to another in the effort to make a living, — running an elevator in one place, marking tags in another, tending a rivet machine in another, etc., etc., — spending years of time and energy in narrow specialization, and getting no adequate, comprehensive understanding of any business or industry.

The union of a broad general culture with an industrial education, including a practical experience broad enough to form a true foundation for specialization in the proper field, possesses an economic and social value that can hardly be overestimated. Yet practically all our children are subjected to the evil of unbalanced specialization, — specialization that is not founded on, or accompanied by, the broad culture and experience that should form its basis and be continued as coördinate factors in a full development,— specialization that is not only unbalanced

162　CHOOSING A VOCATION

and ill-founded, but also in many cases inherently narrow, inefficient, and hurtful in itself.

Most of the children who leave school early specialize on narrow industrial lines, and most of those who remain in school specialize on book learning. Book work should be balanced with industrial education; and working children should spend part time in culture classes and industrial science. Society should make it possible for every boy and girl to secure at least a high-school education and an industrial training at the same time. This can be done by the establishment of Public Half-Work High Schools, in which boys and girls can study half of each day, and support themselves by working the other half-day for the public water works, lighting or transportation systems, street department or some other department of the public service, or for private employers.

A city or town can easily make arrangements with merchants, manufacturers, and other private employers, whereby the high-school pupils may have the opportunity to work half-time in many lines of industry. The Women's Educational and Industrial Union of Boston is already carrying on this sort of arrangement with some of the leading merchants of the city, so that the girls in the Union's classes in salesmanship are able to support themselves and get most valuable practical training by working half-time in the stores. Enlightened employers are glad to make such arrangements, realizing the importance to themselves and to the whole community of such advanced industrial and culture training. Some of our agricultural colleges and state universities, especially in the West, afford opportunities for young men and women to earn their living while getting a college education. The University of Cincinnati is an illustrious example. All that is necessary is to extend the methods and principles already in use to the public-school system as a whole, so

CONCLUSIONS 163

that no boy or girl shall be longer debarred from the training of mind and hand, which is the rightful heritage of every child society allows to be born into this complex and difficult world.

Besides the extension of general education and the addition of vocational training, the methods of general culture should be materially modified, if we are to give our boys and girls an adequate preparation for life and work instead of a preparation for passing an examination to get a degree. We should train for ability and character rather than for examinations. And the principal test should be the successful performance of things that have to be done in daily life, rather than the answering of a series of questions about a book or a lecture course. Systematic and scientific training of body and brain, of memory, reason, imagination, inventiveness, care, thoroughness, truth, promptitude, reliability, sympathy, kindliness, persistent industry, etc., etc., is what we need. Education for power; with actual performance, useful work, as the fundamental test. Power in any direction comes from exercise or activity in that direction, together with sufficient development in other directions to give symmetry and balance to the whole. Even the power of sympathy and the sense of justice can be developed by daily exercise, on the same principle that we develop the biceps or the bicycle muscles. Knowledge is excellent; but a man with knowledge only, without the power of original thought and the ability to put his ideas into effective execution, is little better than a book — he contains a record of facts but cannot build or execute. He may not even be up to the book standard of life if he has not learned to express and impart his knowledge. That is why college graduates, even those who stood high in their classes, often fail to make good in business. They are good bookworms, sponges, absorbing machines, but they do not

164   CHOOSING A VOCATION

know how to do things, and have no taste for doing things. They are really unfitted, by their habits of passive absorption, for the active life of the business world. We must train our students to full powers of action, not only in football and other athletic sports, but in the various lines of useful work so far as possible, according to their aptitudes as brought out by scientific tests and varied experience. And we must give our working boys the powers of thought and verbal expression that come with general culture. And we must do all this in the formative period, before the progressive hardening of the system has taken the bloom from development and modifiability.

Youth is the period of plasticity and rapid development, in which the foundation should be laid both for an all-round culture and for special vocational power. The fluidity of youth is shown in the fact that practically 75 per cent of the infant's body is water, while only 58.5 per cent of the adult's body is liquid. Though some degree of plasticity may be retained to the end, the more fundamental characteristics of a man are generally fixed at twenty-five, and the mental at thirty-five or forty. If you were moulding a statue in plaster of Paris, you would not think it wise to neglect the work or let it drag along half-done till the plastic mass had stiffened into rigidity. It is just as unwise to neglect the opportunities afforded by the plasticity of youth. A year of the period from fifteen to twenty-five is worth more than two years after thirty-five, for formative purposes and the development of power. Youth is the age of brain and heart. The body of an adult is three times as long, on the average, as the infant's body, and the adult's arms are four times and his legs five times as long as the infant's, while his head is only twice the height of the infant's. The brain of the child is so large that it only increases in weight four times in the growth to maturity, while the heart increases thirteen

CONCLUSIONS   165

times, and the body more than twenty times. The weight of the brain at birth is 12.29 percent of the total weight, while at twenty-five the weight of the brain is only 2.16 per cent of the whole, — nearly six times as much brain weight for the infant as for the adult in proportion to the total weight. As you leave your youth the rapidity of development diminishes, as well as the proportion of brain, and the plasticity or capacity for modification and acquirement of new abilities. The infant at birth is five million times as large as the original germ cell. In the first year the growth is about threefold. Then the rate of development decreases till about the eleventh year, when a period of rapid growth begins, reaching its maximum speed as a rule somewhere between the fourteenth and the nineteenth year, and gradually tapering off to the milder movement of comparative maturity after twenty-five.

In this plastic period of rapid growth, this age of brain and heart, society should guarantee to every child a thorough all-round development of body, mind, and character, and a careful planning of and adequate preparation for some occupation, for which, in the light of scientific testing and experiment, the youth seems best adapted, or as well adapted as to any other calling which is reasonably available. If this vital period is allowed to pass without the broad development and special training that belong to it, no amount of education in after years can ever redeem the loss. Not till society wakes up to its responsibilities and its privileges in this relation shall we be able to harvest more than a fraction of our human resources, or develop and utilize the genius and ability that are latent in each new generation. When that time does come, education will become the leading industry, and a vocation bureau in effect will be a part of the public-school system in every community, — a bureau provided with every facility that science can devise for the testing of the senses and capacities, and the whole physical, intellectual, and emotional make-up of the child, and with experts trained as carefully for the work as men are trained to-day for medicine and the law.